Think Simple

Think Simple

How Smart Leaders
Defeat Complexity

Ken Segall

Portfolio/Penguin

An imprint of Penguin Random House LLC
375 Hudson Street
New York, New York 10014

Hardcover ISBN 9781591847502
E-book ISBN 9780698180864

Printed in the United States of America
10   9   8   7   6   5   4   3   2   1

Book design by Daniel Lagin

For Jeremy:
I'll get you to Australia one day,
I swear. Had to write a book first.

Contents

Think Simple

Introduction
Simplicity Isn't Simple

Simplicity is one of the most deceptive concepts on earth.

It's arguably the most potent weapon in business—attracting customers, motivating employees, outthinking competitors, and creating new efficiencies. Yet rarely is it as simple as it looks.

Simplicity takes work.

But, as more and more companies around the world are discovering, the ROI on simplicity can be astonishingly high. Simplicity can power a company to amazing growth or revive a company that's become mired in complexity.

While clients and customers see simplicity as an end result, the reality is that it's so much more. It's a philosophy and a methodology, and it can be implemented at every level of an organization. It can transform a company internally and change the way it's perceived by others.

I often feel like I have the easiest job on earth. It's not like I have to convince the world that simplicity is a good thing. We all know that. Obviously, customers are attracted to companies that offer simpler solutions. Employees are more motivated when the work environment is less complex, and prospects respond best to communications that register quickly and clearly.

These things are a given. The challenge is this: How exactly does a company make the journey "from here to simplicity"? That's what this book is all about.

Becoming an Agent of Simplicity

It's no wonder complexity has become so entrenched in this world. It's had a few thousand years to dig in. One could say that complexity is actually a side effect of civilization.

The more we discover, the more we invent, the more we advance, the more complicated life becomes. Which is ironic, given that so many innovations are meant to simplify.

It would be convenient to blame the current state of the world's complexity on technology, but we have to face the facts. The real culprit is us. We're human. It's in our DNA to prefer simpler things, yet we so often open the door to complexity.

That's because being complicated is easy. Making things simpler is the more challenging task, and one that is often neglected. Nowhere is this more true than in the world of business.

As our companies grow, we dream up new ways to manage, organize, communicate, and compete. We do it all with the best of intentions, but things get complicated along the way. Internal structures grow more complex. Product lines expand. Processes proliferate. Levels of hierarchy multiply. People start defending their turf. Meetings begin to consume our days.

We do it all in the name of achieving consistent, repeatable success, but we pay the price by sacrificing simplicity. Business just isn't as frictionless as it once was. That beautiful focus present at a company's inception becomes nothing more than a plaque on the wall or a dedication in a fifty-page employee manual.

If the signs of complexity are present in your business, you're not alone. In fact, you're among the vast majority of companies in this world. The good news is, where there is complexity, there is also opportunity.

You can become an agent of simplicity. You can put your company on a course to undo the complexity that has taken root over time. Or, if your company is currently enjoying the fruits of simplicity, you can help lay the groundwork to ensure that it can resist the forces of complexity that will inevitably appear.

My previous book, *Insanely Simple*, was based on observations gained from twelve years working as Steve Jobs's advertising agency creative director, first with NeXT and then with Apple. I saw firsthand that Steve looked at everything through the lens of simplicity. His obsession with simplicity was not only visible in Apple's products, but you could see it in the way the company organized, innovated, advertised, sold at retail, and provided customer service.

In practice, simplicity was Steve's most powerful business weapon. It helped Apple distinguish its products and create entirely new product categories, and it put distance between Apple and its competitors. But, while Apple is a terrific example of a company that has been propelled by the power of simplicity, it is hardly alone.

Heroes of Simplicity

Inspired by the ways Apple has benefited from the power of simplicity, I set out to find other companies that were traveling this path. I wanted to learn more about the thinking of their leaders. I felt that if I could chronicle the experiences of those who have successfully simplified, it would be an invaluable guide for those who would like to do the same.

This book is the result of my journey into simplicity in companies around the world.

Over the course of three years, I searched for the smartest, most inventive spokespeople for simplicity that I could find. I landed some of my interviews the old-fashioned way: I begged. I also picked the brains of former colleagues and clients and latched onto a terrific researcher who provided a treasure chest of possibilities.

I will not hide the fact that I had a blast doing the research. I felt privileged to meet a number of leaders I have long admired and to have my eyes opened in unexpected ways by the leaders of some truly fascinating companies.

Many of the "heroes of simplicity" profiled in this book wouldn't be found on your list of usual suspects. By the time I'd finished my research, I'd had conversations with over forty men and women from a wide range of industries in many countries. I'd talked to leaders from companies big and small, established and up-and-coming, famous and under the radar. I'd looked at businesses local, national, and international.

Each leader has a fascinating point of view about how simplicity has helped improve his or her company and set it apart from competitors. Each is unique, yet, as you'll find, many display interesting similarities.

From Jerry Greenfield you'll hear how Ben & Jerry's grew from local to global without losing its focus and simple values. From the CEO of one of Australia's biggest banks you'll hear how simplicity is attracting new customers. From former Apple senior VP Ron Johnson you'll hear how a simple idea aligned the team creating the worldwide network of Apple Stores.

You'll discover how simplicity influences the CEOs of The Container Store and Whole Foods. You'll get insights on simplification from the worlds of fashion, automobiles, entertainment, and technology. You'll even get inside the blue heads of the Blue Man Group, who developed a business strategy to defeat complexity before it could take root.

My goal is to use the experience and success of these leaders to give you an advantage before you even start to simplify—whatever business you're in. The thinking of these people will inspire you to look at your company in a different light. Hopefully, a simpler light.

The Universal Advantage

Obviously, start-ups and small companies have an easier time leveraging the power of simplicity. It's the nature of small groups to have greater focus, as they haven't yet had to deal with the creeping effects of complexity that show up over time.

The challenge for these types of companies is to understand the importance of their simpler ways and hold on to them as they get bigger.

For big companies, simplification presents a world of challenges. Many believe that simplifying a global company with thousands of employees is a lost cause. Not true. It isn't easy, but it is hardly impossible. Again, Apple serves as a good example.

In 1997, when Steve Jobs returned to the company after eleven years in exile, he found a global organization in miserable shape. The innovative, spritely Apple he had known had become bloated and mediocre. The company was only ninety days from bankruptcy.

We all know what happened next. Steve performed a major overhaul and turned Apple into the most valuable company on earth in a span of only fourteen years. Steve was many things: visionary, dreamer, innovator, and natural leader. However, he was not a magician. He changed Apple by taking a commonsense, one-step-at-a-time approach.

He turned an unfocused organization into a place where everyone understood the journey ahead and the part they were to play. He simplified the corporate structure, he simplified the product line, and he simplified the marketing. As Steve himself would explain after the company became a global powerhouse, Apple was "the world's biggest start-up."

Not every business leader is a Steve Jobs. But every business leader can be inspired by Apple's transformation and realize that spectacular gains can be realized by leveraging the power of simplicity.

The truth is, every company stands to benefit from simplification. In companies where simplicity can't be built into the products, it can certainly be built into the organization—in the processes that form its backbone, the way it communicates internally, and the way it connects with customers.

Perception Versus Reality

The irony of simplicity is that it often appears to be something it is not.

For example, a product, service, or website might appear to be simple, but creating it likely involved passionate debate and hard work by a devoted group over a long period of time. Customers don't see that. What they see is the simplicity that results.

So the truth is, there is really no such thing as simplicity. What we're talking about is the *perception* of simplicity. It's what the customer takes away from the experience.

Few can explain the technology beneath the display of their trusty tablet, yet what they see is the simplest PC in history. Automobiles incorporate complex systems few can comprehend, but driving is simple. The workings of the power grid are beyond the comprehension of most, yet anyone can flip a light switch.

Even something as wonderfully simple as ice cream conceals its inner complexity. When I sat down with Jerry Greenfield, cofounder of Ben & Jerry's, "perception versus reality" was one of the first topics that came up.

> *What strikes me when talking about simplicity is that in some ways Ben & Jerry's is a little bit the opposite. We've chosen to do certain things that are more complex than others are willing to do—or even try to do. Our hallmark is a selection of interesting flavors with big chunks of cookies, candy, and swirls.*
>
> *Your classic ice cream machinery is only designed to handle small bits of things. We were kind of the first to figure out how to add in those big chunks. It's very complicated to do this on a large scale, but to our customers it looks simple.*

That's the wonder of simplicity. It may be nothing more than perception, but it has the power to drive a business.

Faster, Better, Cheaper—Pick Three

One of the first computer ads I ever wrote was for IBM Personal Computers. Back then I had precious little experience to draw upon and a serious lack of confidence, so I was eager to absorb everything I could.

Lesson number one came from a manic commercial director in Los Angeles. At the start of preproduction he stood at the head of the table and delivered a speech to the agency creative team, producers, account managers, and IBM marketing people.

Calm at first, his speech soon escalated into a full-scale rant that was scary enough for me to vividly remember decades later. His point was that he, as the director, had to juggle three things: quality, cost, and speed. The bad news was that we could choose only two.

"Take your choice!" he screamed. "If you want me to shoot this commercial fast and cheap, fine, but it isn't going to be great. If you want a great spot fast, you're going to have to spend more." And so on.

To be honest, I don't remember which two we chose. Since that's one commercial I haven't shared with a soul since, I'm thinking it was quality that got short shrift.

For some time I believed this was a basic rule of business in general, and not just advertising production. However, several years and several clients later, I began an association with someone who proved that it's only a rule if you allow it to be a rule: Steve Jobs. Time and time again, Steve demonstrated that quality, speed, and cost can coexist quite nicely. The secret is to not let complexity get in the way.

Steve preferred to work with a small group of smart people, and he was a tireless protector of the creative thinking that came out of that group. With fewer people involved and a lack of overanalysis, we spent less money. Without endless rounds of approvals and revisions, we created faster. And the work that resulted was of award-winning quality.

We had unrestricted access to the ultimate decision maker (Steve), and we never even dreamed of subjecting our advertising to focus-group testing.

And guess what—despite the fact that we had none of the elaborate checks and balances in our system that were mandatory in the worlds of Dell, Intel, and Microsoft, we created better advertising. Apple consistently captured people's attention with interesting, entertaining ads that memorably communicated what it had to offer.

It's no coincidence that this level of work resulted from a system that was infinitely less complicated.

Don't let anyone tell you that "faster, better, and cheaper" is unattainable. But do bear in mind that it can never be achieved within an organization that clings to complicated processes.

The Science of Simple

Simplicity plays a role in every business. The problem is, it's not always given the attention it deserves. I believe that's because many people take simplicity for granted and don't feel a compelling need to understand how and why it impacts their business.

I spoke to a digital design firm in London called Foolproof, which has dived deeply into the nature of simplicity, with a goal of creating websites that better connect with customers.

Foolproof's partners and cofounders, Tom Wood and Peter Ballard, came from the world of Virgin Money, a progressive consumer champion brand that was wrestling with a problem. Its marketing team had succeeded in getting people to the company's website, but visitors weren't buying much when they got there.

As part of the Virgin team, Tom and Peter ran some cheap and easy tests to see if small changes to their site might have an effect on the conversion rate. What they found was that even small changes in page layout, typography, color, content, and design could have a *huge* effect. In this they sensed a business opportunity and created Foolproof, which bills itself as an "experience design agency."

A small company at first, Foolproof has now expanded beyond the UK's borders. Its client list includes major technology companies, banks, airlines, and media companies. These are the types of organizations that often find themselves with a "complication in the system." That is, they tend to overcomplicate the experience customers have on their website.

Foolproof's job is to simplify that experience. It does so by promoting the concept of "flow," a theory put forward by Hungarian psychologist Mihaly Csikszentmihalyi. His thesis is that when you're in a process that creates flow, you don't know you're in a process because it's so intuitive.

Driving a car is a good example, says Tom. When you don't know how to drive a car, it seems complicated. There are many things to be aware of, and the consequences of screwing something up range from frustrating to life-threatening. But once you know how to drive a car, it's quite simple. You can even talk while you're doing it. You're in a state of flow.

Applying the idea of flow to interaction design, Foolproof tries to create a journey that is so beautifully clear that visitors aren't conscious of the design or the process. They're simply having a good experience.

Psychologically the state of flow is a form of happiness. You know what you've done, you know what to do next, and you know where this is going. As Tom explains it, you're content to live in this moment and you don't seek distractions.

In creating a state of flow, one must not only create the positive experience— one must avoid the negative and distracting experiences. Generally speaking, you need to avoid such states as anxiety, worry, and boredom. Looking at design this way, anything you do that increases the sense of flow adds to the positive experience. But when you give someone the tiniest split second where you break that bubble, you put the flow at risk.

I'm quite enamored with the concept of flow. It's the closest I've seen to a scientific explanation of why simplicity works. Flow is an excellent goal for any business trying to engage customers, and it's useful in creating a more productive work environment for employees as well. But like all good things, it takes dedication to achieve.

The Road to Simple

The path to a simpler business is marked fairly well, but since every business is unique, there is no standard formula. You'll need to do a bit of improvising.

That said, as I interviewed my subjects, a number of themes arose that are applicable to just about every business. Each chapter in this book is devoted to one of those themes—nine in all. By the book's end you'll find it easier to put together your own road map to simplicity.

Be prepared, because you may well encounter resistance as you put the theories into practice. Try not to let the naysayers depress you, and certainly don't let them sway you. There will always be people uncomfortable with change and those who will work to thwart you, consciously or subconsciously.

This is where you may need to channel a bit of Steve Jobs. There were principles on which Steve would never compromise. Simplicity was one of them, and his belief in simplicity helped turn Apple into such a spectacular success. That kind of tenacity will serve you well.

This is the start of your road to simple. Safe travels.

Chapter 1
Simplicity Is on a Mission

The foundational building block of just about every exceptional company is its mission. And some of the most successful companies in the world have been built upon a very simple mission.

Amazon is a good example. Years ago Jeff Bezos came up with three simple words that captured the essence of the company: "One click away." It almost sounded like a campaign theme line, but it went much deeper than that. This phrase neatly summed up the most important benefit to everyone who visited the Amazon site. You were one click away from finding just about any product on earth and one click away from exceptional customer service. Once you turned on the feature, you'd even see the "Buy Now With 1-Click" option every time you shopped.

At every opportunity, Bezos reminded the company of the importance of those words. Every initiative ultimately had to serve that grander purpose.

At the highest level, the mission is a company's reason for being. It keeps a company focused on the path forward, uniting employees in a common quest. It acts as a guideline for products, services, communications, marketing, and virtually every important decision a company might face. It also serves as a guardrail that prevents a company from veering off its intended path.

Some companies articulate their mission with a formal set of words, using them to rally the troops and train new recruits. Others have a mission that is so well integrated into their business that it's rarely spoken aloud yet is deeply felt throughout the organization. Either way, the mission helps the entire workforce understand why they do what they do. It inspires and motivates.

In his book *Start with Why* and in his TED talk "How Great Leaders Inspire Action," Simon Sinek offers what he calls "the world's simplest idea." He observes that the most inspiring companies communicate the "why" of what they do, rather than just hype a product and tell people how it works. Companies that have a mission—those that stand for something—make a deeper and more lasting impression on their customers. By communicating the why, they gain importance and relevance—and an advantage over their competitors.

The act of crystallizing the why is an effective simplifier in itself, as it forces one to shed excess verbiage to get to the essence of the company's motivation. There is a principle at work here that will appear at several points in this book. That is, there is tremendous power in the ability to effectively distill. Distilling information to its essence makes an idea easier to remember and harder to forget.

A complex mission may appease different points of view within the company, but it's less likely to create focus among employees, and more likely to confuse customers. It's like flying five flags instead of one.

A good example of an unfocused mission statement can be found at McDonald's. Its mission references a complex global strategy called the "Plan to Win." It's difficult to assign all the blame for the company's overly complicated menu and poor financial performance in recent years to the lack of a clear, concise mission—but this lack certainly doesn't help.

When people talk about companies driven by a mission, it's not unusual to find Apple in the conversation. We've all come to know the modern, successful Apple, but when the company was withering from complexity back in the late 1990s, the mission became a powerful tool for much-needed simplification.

The Transformational Power of the Mission

In 1997 Apple acquired NeXT, the company Steve had started when he was driven from Apple eleven years earlier. Steve was part of the package, agreeing to become an adviser to Apple's then-CEO Gil Amelio. Shortly after the acquisition, Gil trotted Steve onstage at a company event to explain how NeXT technology was going to enable Apple's great leap forward.

Knowing how the story ends for both Steve and Gil, it's simultaneously informative and entertaining to watch the YouTube video of this event.* At the very start Amelio appears humbled by the fact that Steve is received with wildly enthusiastic applause, and Steve looks very moved by it. Steve also seems a bit restrained because he knows that, at least for the moment, he is playing a side role in the Gil Amelio show.

In the first seconds of his address, Steve thought it was important to focus on Apple's mission. On the screen behind him he put up the following slide:

> MISSION: *Provide relevant, compelling solutions that customers can only get from Apple.*

These words illuminated Apple's path forward at this critical fork in the road, when Apple was barely breathing. Following his successful coup not long afterward, having been appointed "interim CEO," Steve went about the business of remodeling the company and its product line exactly as his mission described. Apple became far simpler as a result, laying the groundwork for amazing growth ahead.

While a company's mission is critical, that doesn't mean it's carved in stone. Companies evolve over the years, and their mission statements need

---

* https://youtu.be/4QrX047-v-s.

to evolve in tandem. For Apple the transformation from computer company to consumer electronics company was an important turning point. Even its name changed, from Apple Computer, Inc. to Apple Inc. Its mission was refined to be more about innovation and defining the future.

Another important turning point for Apple was the creation of the retail Apple Store. Building a chain of stores required hundreds of decisions, from basic concept and architecture to locations, store layout, and hiring. The Apple Stores would offer not only products but also advice, training, support, and—via its staff—a healthy dose of Apple enthusiasm. This retail effort would require a mission of its own.

Steve Jobs recruited Ron Johnson to help conceive and build the Apple Stores we know today. I spoke to Ron about how the idea of an Apple Store grew from a simple concept to one of the greatest successes in retail history, with hundreds of locations worldwide. He explained that the key moment for the Apple Store actually came with the development of its own mission.

The team worked hard to develop a statement that would align with Apple's overall mission and also lay the foundation for a compelling in-store experience. It would be the guide for everything that happened inside the stores. It had to be easy to remember, Ron said, so it could be socialized throughout the retail organization.

Apple is about creating products that change people's lives, right? So for the Apple Store mission, we came up with one simple phrase: "Enrich lives." The entire store, and the experience in the store, would be designed to enrich not only the lives of the customers but the employees as well.

The phrase "Enrich lives" didn't appear in any signage or in any of the store collateral. Yet this mission was ever present in the development and operation of the stores. It was the test applied to every part of the customer experience, from store design to employee conduct to services offered. If an idea wasn't consistent with the concept of enriching lives, it was rejected.

The mission was a major factor in making one of the most important decisions of all—the locations where the stores would be built. If your stores are about enriching people's lives, says Ron, you can't make people go out of their way to find you. Logically, then, the company chose to build Apple Stores in malls, where they would be easily accessible during everyday shopping trips.

The mission was also top of mind when it came to the issue of how to fix customers' products if they ever needed service. Ron is credited with hatching the idea of the Genius Bar. Here, customers would feel like they were getting the attention of the smartest Apple person in town. That would not only enrich the lives of the customers, but it would also enrich the lives of the geniuses themselves. Ron explains:

> *The Genius Bar enriched the employee's life because it recognized his or her level of expertise. "Genius" was a title employees coveted. What if we just had a repair department? Well, I don't want to work in a repair department. But if I can be the Apple Genius in Minneapolis—that's a more fulfilling job, right?*

Ron and his team put major effort into creating the ideal profile of those who would be employed at the Apple Store. With "Enrich lives" as a guideline, they looked for smart, interesting people who were not only passionate about technology and the Apple brand but also eager to share their expertise.

> *Now people are working for Apple, they have a job with meaning, and they're here to serve others—which so many people love to do.*
>
> *Talk about the power of simplicity. All that came out of one very simple idea: Enrich lives. It described what Steve was doing with Apple, and so with this philosophy the Apple Stores were the perfect representation of the brand.*

The mission continued to guide decisions as more stores were opened around the world. It all came together to create a retail success story that will likely be studied for decades.

Of course, the mission of the Apple Stores was successful in part because it reflected an Apple philosophy that had been built over many years. But a clear mission is every bit as valuable to a company that's in its earliest stages.

Finding a Mission That Scales

Jeff Fluhr is the cofounder of StubHub, an online ticket marketplace that operates in the United States and the UK. He started the company in 2000 and just seven years later sold it to eBay for a reported $310 million. He is in many ways the perfect spokesman for the new generation of technology entrepreneurs—he had a compelling idea, launched an Internet-based service, and then successfully grew the company to stratospheric heights as its popularity took root.

Like many start-ups, StubHub didn't exactly follow a rule book. Jeff makes it clear that he did not start the business with a mission statement in mind. However, as StubHub grew, he changed his tune about the value of having one.

> *When we first started StubHub, I was a very young CEO and entrepreneur, about twenty-five years old. I'd actually never even worked at an operating company before. So I hadn't really seen a model of how people had created mission statements for their companies, and I discounted that kind of thing.*
>
> *Now I've come to realize that the mission statement can be a powerful tool. It can align people internally, and externally it can help people better understand what you are doing.*

As StubHub grew into a company with hundreds of employees, Jeff brought on senior executives with more business experience than he and cofounder Eric Baker had. One of these organizationally savvy people suggested that if the business were to become as big as its ambition, StubHub should seriously consider having a mission statement. It was one of those "oh, right" moments.

Jeff and his team set about creating a mission and ultimately discovered that one already existed inside their theme line: "Where fans buy and sell tickets." Whether you were a buyer or a seller, you came to StubHub because you were a fan of music or sports. Jeff explains that the simple idea of serving the fan became the driver of StubHub's business.

> *Verbalizing our mission not only gave the company more focus, but it was also helpful in terms of just speaking to the world about what we were doing. We were about the fans—and therefore we were not about the venues and the teams and the leagues, or the performing artists and the music space and the music industry. We were about the fans. That was really, really important in guiding the company's actions. Without it, StubHub would not have succeeded as it did.*

The mission statement was also critical to growth because it helped the company take on the forces that were aligned against it. In those early days many teams, leagues, and artists spoke out against the idea of reselling a ticket for more than its face value. And there were those who didn't think tickets should be resold at any price.

When legislatures and various factions challenged the legality of StubHub, the company was able to put forward a powerful line of defense. It was able to point to its mission statement and say, "Look, we're all about the fans. In a free country fans have the right to trade tickets and money if both the buyer and seller feel it is in their best interest." StubHub was simply empowering fans to take advantage of free-market economics.

> *Our mission of being about the fan, and about fans having choice and access, really helped to clarify and simplify what we were doing.*

For StubHub, like the Apple Store, the mission influenced every decision moving forward, from new product features to marketing. It helped the company stay focused as it empowered customers with a new and exciting service.

StubHub blazed a trail in its industry. But a clear mission is also a powerful advantage for companies looking for ways to succeed in well-established categories where competition is intense. A unique mission is a guideline for differentiation.

A Simple Mission Stands Out In a Crowd

It's hard enough to get noticed when you're a new player in a category where product features offer a logical means of comparison. It's tougher still when you're in an industry where products are personal, emotional, experiential, and entirely subjective, as they are in the world of fashion.

Joe Fresh, Canada's number two fashion brand, has not only achieved success in its home country but also expanded its presence around the world. The company started with a clear, simple mission: "Fresh fashion at fresh prices." It also happened to work beautifully as the marketing theme.

The force behind Joe Fresh is Joe Mimran, a Canadian entrepreneur with a résumé in fashion that dates back to 1976. Joe has a passion for simplicity, not only in fashion but also in the way he runs his business. Joe Fresh was born when Canada's Weston family—whose Loblaws supermarket chain does $35 million worth of business annually—approached Joe with the idea of selling apparel in their supermarkets.

The Westons were eager to have Joe do battle with their main competitor, Walmart. They showed him some of the clothing items Walmart was selling, but Joe wasn't interested in going toe to toe with the giant retailer.

> I said, "You know, that's not what I do. If I'm going to work with you, I'd like to propose my idea of what it should be." The name "Joe Fresh"—in fact, the whole idea of "fresh"—came from the idea of clothes being sold in a food store. Fresh fashion. It made sense.

Because the line would be carried in a supermarket at first, Joe felt that the pricing needed to be surprisingly affordable ("fresh prices") and the clothes needed to be appealing in a different way ("fresh fashion"). The colors had to be "tasty"—no dead colors and certainly no black, regardless of what the fashion trends might be.

The mission was evident in every discussion about the new brand. Determined to keep the proposition simple and not deviate from the mission, Joe didn't want to get involved in markdowns. He went with everyday low pricing from the start.

The mission also powered the marketing strategy. Joe believed it was important to keep the brand image crystal clear. He thought it would only confuse people if Joe Fresh ran ads introducing people to a hot new fashion brand and then urged them to see it for themselves in a supermarket. That would have been a head-scratcher. Instead, Joe did something few marketers would do in any circumstance: He advertised the brand without telling viewers where it could be found. There was no mention of Loblaws at all.

Unsurprisingly, there was debate over the wisdom of introducing the brand this way. But there is no denying that the idea was bold: sell the brand first, marketing the new fashion line aggressively, and then let shoppers be surprised when they "discovered" it in the supermarkets. As Joe explains it, people were going to be surprised by Joe Fresh one way or the other. Either they would see a commercial that suggested they could find fashionable clothing in a supermarket or they would unexpectedly find the hot new fashion brand they had seen on TV while doing their food shopping. Joe felt that the latter option would spring a delightful surprise upon Loblaws shoppers.

Joe Fresh initially debuted in forty Loblaws stores. It took time for some people to get used to the Joe Fresh concept, but the brand—and the way the brand articulated the mission—won people over. As Joe puts it:

> *What we created was this unique idea of clothing in a food store, brand integrity, and quality that you would never expect, at mass price points.*

Joe attributes the success of Joe Fresh to a compelling brand vision, integrity in product development, and that crystal-clear mission. As his story illustrates, a clear mission is a good start for a company, but what accelerated the growth of Joe Fresh was finding creative ways to bring the mission to life.

Now, common sense would suggest that a growing company would have one mission, and that all of its actions would align with that mission. That was certainly the case with Apple and Joe Fresh.

However, I came across one company that has developed a different kind of mission. Though the idea might seem counterintuitive, this company's simplicity is born of the fact that its mission is deeper than most.

A Mission Simplifies Big Beliefs

Fans of Ben & Jerry's have an uncomplicated understanding of the company. They see rich, creamy ice cream with fantastic ingredients, a familiar graphic style across all of the company's packaging, and a feisty spirit that has not faded over time. But many would also point out another important aspect of the company: Ben & Jerry's has a conscience. It's active in social causes.

At the highest level the company does have a singular mission statement—"Contributing to positive change in the world"—but this is actually the sum of three distinct missions. When I sat down with co-founder Jerry Greenfield, he explained how this multipart mission has guided the company's business.

Over time we came up with a three-part mission. We have our product mission, our financial mission, and our social mission.

All three of these missions are equally important and interrelated. It's not enough to make money if we're not doing the social mission. Because if we don't do the social mission, we haven't succeeded in our overall mission.

Each part of Ben & Jerry's three-part mission contributes to the company's quest to create positive change in the world—promoting the use of wholesome ingredients, offering career growth for employees, and improving the quality of life locally, nationally, and internationally. The three-part mission adds a layer of complexity to Ben & Jerry's operations that its competitors don't have to deal with. At the same time, the three-part mission keeps the company on track and sets Ben & Jerry's apart from other ice cream makers.

Ben & Jerry's wasn't founded with a one- or three-part mission in mind. Rather, its mission evolved organically over time.

Jerry and cofounder Ben Cohen had been close friends since their junior high school days. Ben had dropped out of college and tried to become a potter but soon found that no one wanted to buy his pottery. Jerry had gone to college as a premed student, only to find himself rejected by medical schools. Together the two had to confront a question that greets many of us after graduation: What's next?

In 1978 the pair moved to Burlington, Vermont, and, without any business training whatsoever, decided to start a little homemade ice cream parlor in a renovated garage. They learned how to make ice cream from a five-dollar correspondence course. Jerry recalls:

Our goal was to just have a little community business. Be on the corner, have people come in, whatever. There was nothing more than that. There was no grander mission. Our goal was to earn twenty thousand bucks a year.

At first Ben and Jerry had no choice but to be a small and local business, because they were extremely limited in their ability to create the product. They didn't have the financial resources, they had little knowledge of the industry, and "manufacturing" was limited to the quantities of unique flavors they could mix by hand in the back room.

Ultimately they invented methods to produce their unique products in greater quantities, and that's when things started to change. Limited by the brevity of ice cream season in often-freezing Vermont, Ben and Jerry needed to expand beyond Burlington if the business was to grow.

As the company got bigger, the founders came up with their version of a mission statement. They referred to it as the "core principles." These principles included such statements as "Business has a responsibility to give back to the community" and "If it's not fun, why do it?" Ben & Jerry's was guided by the core principles until the three-part mission was formalized in 1988.

> *There came a point where we began to realize we weren't little ice cream guys anymore. We were business guys. But because we started as we did, we recognized the role that business plays in the community and in society. That's when we formally developed the three-part mission. I think we wrote our mission statement about ten years into the business.*

This mission has driven Ben & Jerry's ever since, to the point where it would be difficult to imagine the company without it.

The founders' social consciousness led to the formation of the Ben & Jerry's Foundation, which is active in many causes. The foundation, to which the company makes donations, operates independently from Ben & Jerry's. It accepts grant applications, and the decisions on those grants are made by volunteer employee groups. The idea is that those who help generate the profit should have some say in where it goes.

The social mission has taught the company that being successful does not necessitate appealing to everyone. More often it's the sharply focused company, the one that's "on a mission," that stands apart from its competitors. Ben & Jerry's no more needs to appeal to buyers of dollar-a-gallon ice cream than Apple needs to appeal to users of ninety-nine-dollar smartphones.

It's when customers identify with the company's mission that they become more deeply connected.

Simplicity Starts Here

One might assume that a typical modern company has a mission or core idea that guides its behaviors, even if it's not formally articulated or celebrated. Yet that is often far from the reality.

In *Insanely Simple* I shared stories of two iconic companies that struggled with their mission statements. In one anecdote I described the experience of a Microsoft advertising executive who attended an internal marketing meeting where some of the company's most senior executives were unable to explain what Microsoft stood for. In the other I shared my own experience working with Dell when orders were given to create a new brand campaign. There too a number of senior executives were unable to articulate their company's mission.

It's startling that global powers like Microsoft and Dell can wrestle with the idea of a mission. But it's also proof that even the most powerful and visible companies can lose sight of simplicity's most basic lessons. Without a coherent, meaningful mission, it's easy to lose focus. The absence of a clear mission often results in the splintering of a company's resources.

In their early days both Microsoft and Dell had distinct and powerful missions, and their products were perfectly aligned. Microsoft aimed to put a computer on every desk. Dell aimed to make computers affordable and customizable. Yet both were unable to fend off the forces of complexity as they grew larger, and their missions became hazy.

Ask anyone on the street what Nike stands for and you'll hear about celebrating athletics. Ask about BMW and you'll hear about performance and luxury. Ask about Apple and you'll hear about innovation and design. However, if you ask people about Dell and Microsoft, you'll probably get a hundred different answers. Even worse, you could ask that question *inside* those companies and still be left wondering.

Having a clear and simple mission is the single most important thing a company can do in the name of simplification. But having a mission is only one part of the puzzle—another challenge is bringing it to life.

Chapter 2
Simplicity Is in the Air

Critical parts of a company can be seen, studied, and evaluated objectively. These include such things as the physical office space, internal processes, org charts, and the products and services that ultimately reach customers. Each component has an impact on a company's ability to operate more simply or present a simpler choice in the marketplace.

But there is something else that's every bit as important to creating a simpler organization. It doesn't have physical substance, so it's far more difficult to measure. It's the culture that exists inside the company and how it is shaped by and supports the company's values.

Culture is unique to every organization, be it in a single location or a network of offices around the city, country, or world. It has an impact on the way employees go about their jobs, get motivated, make decisions, communicate, and interact with customers. And it's pervasive. It shows up in memos, meetings, projects, and products. You might even find clues about a company's culture on the menu board in its cafeteria.

If the mission is the company's defining quest, then the culture provides the framework that guides people to achieve the mission. It rewards decisions and behaviors that push the company in the right direction. It ensures that newly arrived employees absorb "the way we do things here." For example, employees at Whole Foods are immersed in a culture devoted to healthier living, which is reflected in the way they interact with customers. It also helps them participate more knowledgeably in corporate decision making. We'll look more closely at Whole Foods a bit later.

A strong culture also polices itself, expelling those who don't fit in. One vivid example of this can be found in the story of John Browett, who was hired by Apple in 2012 as its senior vice president of retail. John had previously been the accomplished CEO of the Dixons retail chain in the UK, yet he lasted a mere nine months at Apple. His desire to squeeze more profit out of the already ultraprofitable Apple Stores led him to cut the number of store employees and the hours they worked, despite the fact that an abundance of help was one of the Apple Stores' greatest lures. John didn't absorb Apple's culture or its mission, or the importance of customer service to that mission—so the antibodies of the Apple culture attacked the foreign body.

Simplicity is sometimes part of the culture from the beginning. Other times a company must instill simplicity in a culture that has grown complicated over time.

Apple is actually an example of both. It had a culture of simplicity at its birth, before it grew unfocused and complicated. Then, following a certain founder's return, its culture of simplicity became stronger than ever.

Values Guide Behaviors

The combination of unique values and the degree to which each value is emphasized defines a company's culture. That's why you encounter totally different environments when you move from one company to another, even if your new home is in the same industry.

One can often see a company's values reflected in its products, its behaviors, and the types of decisions it makes.

I have a somewhat unique perspective on the culture of Apple, as I served as a creative director for its ad agency, first under the John Sculley regime and then again when Steve Jobs returned to the company in 1997. In effect, I witnessed a tale of two Apples.

When I dealt with Sculley's Apple, the experience was somewhat like my experiences interacting with other global companies. It was formal and complex, requiring multiple levels of approvals before any action could be taken. From all reports this atmosphere didn't change much during the reigns of the two CEOs who followed Sculley.

When Steve Jobs returned to the company in 1997, it was difficult for him to recognize the company he'd left eleven years earlier. Its values had changed. In Steve's eyes the culture had evolved in some unsettling ways. It had that "big company" feel he had always fought against.

It followed that Steve wanted to reorient the culture to support his mission to make products that only Apple could create. To do this, he sought to reinforce the values that had driven Apple to change the world in its earlier days, including innovation, design, and simplicity.

You probably remember Steve's first effort to transform the culture, though you might have mistaken it for an advertising campaign: *Think different*.

Steve asked his ad agency, of which I was a part, to create a campaign that would tell the world that the innovative spirit of Apple was alive and well. To set the stage for Apple's comeback from a few years of miserable performance, we needed to make a statement.

In a matter of weeks the *Think different* campaign was born. In this campaign Apple celebrated the lives of people who had made a real difference in our world, in science, music, film, business, and other endeavors. The idea was that our choice of heroes would reflect the values of Apple itself.

Yes, this campaign was aimed at Apple's current and potential customers, and would serve as a launching pad for future products. But it was also aimed directly at Apple's employees, with a goal of reigniting the culture that had flourished in the company's early years.

On the day the *Think different* campaign was launched, Steve wrote an email to all Apple employees, announcing the new campaign and inviting all to not only embrace the concept but also participate in it. He asked everyone at every level of the company, from receptionists to engineers, to "think different" about the job they did. The words were instructive and empowering.

Those two words captured the spirit of the company and the culture Steve wanted to create. They would have been appropriate had they been posted in the garage where Jobs and cofounder Steve Wozniak had created their very first computer many years earlier, and they would fit perfectly with Steve's reinvented line of Apple products. Steve believed *Think different* would work well as a foundation for rebuilding the company's culture in California and in Apple offices around the world.

During Steve's second stint at the company, values and the culture that formed around them would become more and more critical to keeping the company simple and surviving the challenging times ahead.

In 1998, when Steve had only recently returned to Apple and the company was still fighting to reestablish itself, economic conditions took a dark turn. Many companies suffered as their income and stock prices plummeted. A natural reaction for affected organizations was to circle the wagons and cut their losses. They slashed their workforces. They cut marketing budgets. They pulled back on R&D.

That didn't happen at Apple.

With a nervous company wondering how he would cope with the bleak economic outlook, Steve went onstage in Cupertino to give a talk that was broadcast via closed circuit inside Apple offices worldwide. Given the tenor of the times and pressures being put on the company, what he had to say was a jaw-dropper to many.

Steve announced that Apple would not cut one dollar of its marketing budget. It would not cut one dollar of R&D. It would not fire anyone who didn't deserve it. (I love that qualifier!) Instead, Apple would innovate its way out of this crisis.

Steve Wilhite was Apple's vice president of global marketing communications at that time, and he recalls that vivid demonstration of Apple's values in action. It was because of this trial by fire—and Jobs's reaction to it—that Apple emerged as a stronger, more powerful, and more relevant company. Wilhite recalls this pivotal moment:

> *I'd never seen, under any circumstances, any other industry leader in that environment make that kind of decision and demonstrate that kind of inspiring leadership. And what happened coming out of that? Oh, just the iPod, iPhone, and iPad.*

It's an amazing story, considering that in 1985 Jobs had been forced out of the company largely because he was spending it into oblivion. Here he was, years later, refusing to cut budgets when the company's income was taking a major hit. This time, however, he didn't take any heat for it. He was admired for not wavering on his principles and for protecting the jobs of people who had devoted their lives to the company.

Wilhite says that Apple came through those dark days more innovative— and more relevant—than ever.

> *To be great, you have to have the confidence to be who you are and express yourself in a way that is authentic to you. You stick to your values. If you are not willing to do that, you might be financially successful. You might gain greater short-term value. But you are never going to become iconic. You are never going to make the transition from successful to timeless. Steve Jobs did that.*

Wilhite further points out that while Jobs believed in protecting the company's mission and values, he didn't spend much time pontificating about those things. He preferred to let the products express the company's values.

> *You know, Steve never did an interview about Steve. Never. Not one time. He did interviews about products. He talked about ideas and connecting consumers to ideas. That was his mission, and he never lost focus.*

Often a company's values have a logical connection to its products, such as when a technology company places a high value on innovation. However, values can also have a meaning that goes beyond a company's products.

Ben & Jerry's, for example, became popular because it made great ice cream. Yet its social conscience proved to be a critical part of the culture—uniting the workforce and adding a dimension of pride and service.

Values Transcend the Product

In the first chapter Jerry Greenfield explained the importance of Ben & Jerry's three-part mission and how it propelled the company to its current global success.

One component—the social mission—expresses the values that are so much a part of the company's culture. Over the years these values have helped attract like-minded people and have given employees a sense of fulfillment above and beyond making amazing ice cream.

Ben & Jerry's social conscience has led it to take positions on many different issues, even when those issues have come with risk. In 2014, for example, Ben & Jerry's took a position on a controversial topic in the food industry and in politics. The company came out in support of legislation requiring GMO (genetically modified organism) labeling on all food products. The proposed law would dictate that if a food product contains GMOs, that fact must be stated on its label. The United States has yet to join the more than sixty other nations that currently have such a law. As Jerry explains, the giant food companies are aligned against it.

> It's one of these David and Goliath situations—the people versus the corporations. Ben & Jerry's strongly supports the consumer's right to know, and the big food companies do not.
>
> The truth is, GMO labeling would not be scary at all. Such a label might say something like "May be produced with genetic engineering." That's all. Six words. On the one hand this debate is bizarre, and on the other hand it makes total sense.

It's enough to make Jerry offer his own advice about simplification to his adversaries: Instead of spending all this money fighting the legislation, why not just reallocate some of those millions to telling people that GMOs are a good thing and explaining their benefits, if that's what you believe?

Ben & Jerry's continues to support the legislation, despite the fact that its advocacy puts the company at odds with its parent, Unilever, which is one of those big companies fighting the GMO labeling movement.

But then, Ben & Jerry's support of social causes has always come with liabilities. There are plenty of consumers who refuse to buy the ice cream because they don't agree with the company's positions. Jerry's feeling, though, is that the positives far outweigh the negatives. Within the workplace, the culture ensures that mission and values continue to be talked about. Even if some disagree with the company's position, people are proud to work for a company that cares.

The public's perception of Ben & Jerry's isn't nearly so specific, says Jerry. But it does reflect the values that drive the company.

In general, people have a favorite flavor. They have some unspecific idea that the company does good things. They probably couldn't say exactly what, but they see us as a good company on the right side of things.

How is it that Ben & Jerry's has been able to keep its culture intact, even after it was purchased by Unilever and its brand spread across twenty-seven countries? Think of it as a controlled evolution, in which the company took specific actions to ensure that its values would continuously be reinforced no matter where the future might lead.

As Jerry explained earlier, the company's social mission was institutionalized with the creation of the Ben & Jerry's Foundation. Years later, when Unilever expressed an interest in acquiring the company, extensive discussions took place about how the company's unique culture would fit into Unilever's world. When the deal was finally done, it became known inside the company as "the famous acquisition agreement."

This agreement stipulates that Unilever is responsible for operations and finances, while an independent board of Ben & Jerry's oversees the social mission and integrity of the brand. This agreement is carved in stone, existing in perpetuity. It preserves the company's values and, with the backing of Unilever, provides the necessary resources to grow the brand around the world.

The CEO of Ben & Jerry's is hired and fired by Unilever. And while he reports to Unilever on operational and financial matters, he reports to the board of Ben & Jerry's on the social mission side. His job performance is evaluated by both.

Jerry is a fan of the current CEO, Jostein Solheim, a longtime Unilever employee who has earned the trust of management, knows how to work within the system, and passionately embraces Ben & Jerry's values. In fact, Jostein sounds very much like Jerry when he says, "The world needs dramatic change to address the social and environmental challenges we are facing. Values-led businesses can play a critical role in driving that positive change."

The unique arrangement between these two companies works well because it honors the values of Ben & Jerry's and strengthens its culture. But, Jerry says, the relationship would be difficult for others to replicate.

Other companies can copy Ben & Jerry's ice cream flavors and back their effort with marketing—but none are genuinely and passionately committed to social justice. That's pretty rare in the business world.

On a global scale the challenge for Ben & Jerry's is to express its values in countries where the issues are different from those in the United States. In Australia, for example, Ben & Jerry's started an advocacy campaign for marriage equality. It also undertook a campaign to save the Great Barrier Reef.

The company works hard to be sensitive in the way it advocates, because it does not wish to be perceived as attacking anyone—but, Jerry notes, it wouldn't be Ben & Jerry's if it didn't express its heartfelt beliefs.

The challenge is to make it genuine and real—which it is—and not just be talking about things. But in a new country we can only start by talking about things. And, you know, talk is cheap. So we must demonstrate that we really care.

Again we see that strong values have a simplifying effect. They provide the Ben & Jerry's workforce with purpose—a purpose far greater than churning out amazing new flavors of ice cream.

This is a defining characteristic of companies that benefit from a strong culture. Employees feel like they belong to a special group and believe that they do worthwhile things. Personal fulfillment is as important as financial rewards.

A strong culture, with its ability to focus a workforce on a common goal, is a powerful competitive advantage—even when your product is similar to those of your competitors.

Values Are as Unique as Fingerprints

Most people don't think of the real estate industry the same way they think of the technology industry. But, as John McGrath proves, certain values can be common to both.

John is the founder and CEO of McGrath Limited, a real estate company headquartered in Sydney, Australia. Because of his strict adherence to values, especially an unrelenting commitment to quality, John has been referred to as "the Steve Jobs of real estate."

It's not quite as wacky as it sounds. John handles only premium properties and insists that his employees create a first-class customer experience. As a result of his Jobs-like obsession with high standards, at the end of 2015 McGrath had grown to seventy-eight offices across Australia (twenty-three company owned and fifty-five franchise offices), with sales of more than $10 billion per year.

I randomly picked a McGrath office to visit during my time in Sydney, and I found it to be exactly as advertised—clean, elegant, and furnished to appeal to high-end customers. I had to resist the temptation to buy an apartment on the harbor in Sydney.

I asked John about the role of culture in keeping business simple in an organization spread across so many offices.

He explained that his company would likely sell about ten thousand properties in 2015, making McGrath one of the bigger real estate enterprises in Australia. But in John's view he has a "nice little real estate company with a few great people and a few great clients."

> *People say to me, "It must be hard running a big business." I say, "Look, to be honest, I don't run a big business. I run a tiny business. Apple is a big business. I have thirteen hundred employees—that's bigger than a café but nowhere near as big as Apple."*
>
> *A lot of people think they have a more complex business than they have. More times than not, they actually create the complexity in their mind. I don't think many businesses are complex at all, other than that which their CEOs or founders make them to be.*

Still, John believes that paying heed to simplicity is the key to continued growth and the best way to insulate his company against complexity. In particular he focuses on his company's "purpose"—what we would call its mission.

> *We just have to keep saying, "What is our purpose?" Well, our purpose is to find people who want to sell their property, put a great proposition forward, present their property to the world well, get the best price, and move forward. When you break it down to a simple purpose, all of a sudden it becomes manageable.*

The culture John has created is one dedicated to this purpose. The company's values support the purpose, and values, as we know, drive the culture. McGrath's distinct culture is what differentiates it from industry competitors.

For me, values are the foundation. If you have a strong set of clear values, then obviously your whole team has. If something doesn't fit into your value set, it's not even worthy of discussion. In this company we're committed to respect, integrity, and excellence. If an opportunity, decision, or a process comes along and doesn't fit, I might say, "Why on earth are we having this discussion?"

A strong set of values not only provides a foundation for the culture but also acts as a powerful simplifier. Asked about his most important value, John is quick to answer: "Excellence." When he hears people on his staff say something like "John wouldn't like that," it gives him a good feeling. It's not a sycophantic thing; he takes it as a sign that people truly understand the benchmarks for the organization and are striving to work at that level.

John quotes Tom Peters, author of *In Search of Excellence,* who said, "If not excellence, then what? If not excellence now, then when?" If you're not committing to excellence, John explains, you're actually committing to mediocrity. When you look at it in black and white, those are the only choices.

One example of his commitment to excellence: John demands rigorous and detailed inspections of properties and world-class photography to display them in marketing materials. The general rule at McGrath is that photos must look like they came out of *Architectural Digest*. If the slightest detail is amiss, John insists on a reshoot. The culture uncompromisingly enforces this attention to detail, says John.

When new people join us and they hear things like this, they sometimes react like, "Oh, wow, really?" They quickly find that the answer is "Yes, really." We value excellence and we're committed to excellence in every detail. There's no compromise on that.

Values are never a matter of degree. They are or they aren't. McGrath was founded on its values, it continues to be guided by them, and it stands apart from its competitors because of them. Its culture celebrates them.

It's easy to see how adherence to values can keep a company on an upward trajectory. But strong values also come into play when a deep crisis threatens a company's very existence. In fact, that's often when values do their best work—as demonstrated by one of the world's iconic automobile manufacturers.

Strong Values Inspire Bold Action

When the love of simplicity is instilled in a company's culture, it really can change the way people look at complex things. Often it allows people to solve complicated issues by using common sense to make bold decisions.

Recall the legend of Alexander and the Gordian knot. When people were unable to untie an impossibly convoluted knot, Alexander showed up, examined the situation, and simply sliced through it with his sword. Easy.

Some people have that Alexander-like ability to uncomplicate things. Steve Wilhite, the former Apple marketing chief we met earlier, also led the marketing effort for Volkswagen of America in the early 1990s. He speaks with admiration for then-CEO Bill Young, who, driven by uncompromising values, was able to make bold decisions during challenging times—even though his values ended up costing Young his job.

During Wilhite's tenure with Volkswagen, the company was in distress. With sales having reached 569,000 cars per year in better days, sales in 1992 had dwindled to a mere 49,000 cars—less than 10 percent of what was considered acceptable. Wilhite says that despite the tough times, Bill Young stood by the company's values.

> *Our quality problems were unbelievable. No matter how you measured quality, we were the worst in the industry. Realizing that the next generation of cars would be of even lower quality, Bill Young made a most amazing decision. He said, "We're simply not accepting them."*
>
> *Those cars represented 70 percent of our volume, and Bill just refused them. Imagine Honda saying they're not accepting delivery on the next-generation Accord, or Toyota saying they're not taking the next-generation Camry. That's exactly what Bill did.*

Sometimes it requires bravery to make a decision based on values, and this was certainly one of those times. But Young wasn't finished yet. Since the halting of shipments was his decision and not that of the dealers, he decreed that the dealers would be paid an "implied gross profit" based on what they had sold the previous year. Profits went off a cliff as Volkswagen paid incentives on cars it wasn't selling, cars it wasn't building, and revenues it wasn't generating.

The board accepted Young's decision to refuse delivery of the new cars but ended up firing Young over his decision to pay dealers for cars they didn't sell. In Wilhite's opinion, though, Young's adherence to values became the foundation for a successful rebuilding.

Those two decisions alone didn't save the company, but they allowed us to stay in business in the United States and gave us the opportunity to rebuild. They also drew a line in the sand, flatly stating that low-quality cars were simply unacceptable. Volkswagen would not be in business in the United States today if those bold decisions were not made. Yet they were simple decisions for Bill, because he had the right values. His values let him cut through that Gordian knot.

In contrast to the dedication to values exhibited by Volkswagen of America during Young's tenure, in 2015 the global Volkswagen brand took a major hit when it failed to live up to its values. The company was found to be deceiving government regulators by purposely designing software that would yield better emissions results during testing than when customers drove the cars on the road. By not adhering to its values, Volkswagen shot its brand in the foot, inflicting damage that will likely take years to recover from.

Wilhite was fortunate enough to see strong values at work during his tenures at both Volkswagen of America and Apple. Those companies' values gave them the courage to do what was right—and what is right is ultimately the best business plan, he believes.

*Why aren't other brands like Apple? It's because they don't have the cour-
age of a Steve Jobs to make the right decisions. Steve didn't make decisions
based on testing and research. He relied on his values. Having those strong
values made his decisions much simpler.*

When Wilhite and I talked further about our personal experiences
working with Jobs, "doing the right thing" became the theme of our conversation. Though critics of Steve Jobs might bristle at the idea, our mutual
observation was that this was Jobs's most defining behavior. His insistence
on remaining true to his values, and doing what he felt was right based on
those values, is really what differentiated Apple from its competitors. It's
also what enabled the company to take off at a time when success was
widely considered a long shot.

Of course, every business leader believes he or she is doing the right
thing. But there's a big difference between following the logical side of one's
brain and acting on deeply held beliefs—especially when those beliefs
might not be supported by raw numbers.

The truth is, some of the toughest decisions get easier when they're
guided by a company's values.

Integrity Is a Powerful Value

Early in my advertising life, I came upon a survey that revealed the most
and least respected professions in the United States. At the bottom of the
list, least respected of all, were lawyers and advertising people.

I felt terrible for my parents, because among their three children they
ended up with both a lawyer and an adman. (Somehow one sibling ended
up in the more respectable profession of education.)

Right or wrong, the low ratings of these professions come from a perceived lack of integrity. For that reason I very much enjoyed meeting with
the cofounders of RadicalMedia (often referred to as Radical), creators of
commercials and content for film, television, and Internet. These guys make

a very big deal about integrity—so much so that they describe it as a founding principle of the company and the foundational element of their corporate culture.

Today RadicalMedia is a global company. From its humble beginning as a production house that created commercials, it has expanded over the years to produce a remarkably wide array of media. It's in film (Academy Award–winning documentary *Fog of War* and Grammy Award–winning documentary *Keith Richards: Under the Influence*); it's in television (six seasons of *Iconoclasts* on the Sundance Channel and five seasons of *Oprah's Master Class* on the Oprah Winfrey Network); and it's created major music videos with Katy Perry, Sia, and many more. RadicalMedia also continues to create commercials for such clients as Audi, BMW, Mercedes, Porsche, Ford, GM, CHANEL, GEICO, J.Crew, GE, and a lengthy list of other iconic brands.

Frank Scherma, cofounder and head of Radical's Los Angeles office, remembers a conversation he had with his partner, Jon Kamen, when they launched the company.

> *Jon said that the most important thing we have as producers is our integrity—and that's always been our focus as we've expanded. We need to maintain and protect our integrity, because it really is the driver of our success.*

Jon recalls the same conversation and how it helped get the two founders in sync. Not that theirs is an industry of charlatans, but in the high-pressure, high-budget world of content production, people have been known to do some crazy things. Says Jon:

> *We're sincere about wanting to create great products, but it's this DNA of integrity that has kept us out of trouble. It's kept us true to ourselves and fierce about who and what we are and what we represent. Our longevity in this business is the trust factor we've been able to grow by being consistent with that message.*

Integrity is the core value that drives RadicalMedia's culture. To appreciate how that impacts the company's business, one must understand the many relationships it has to juggle. Traditionally Radical's clients have been advertising agencies, and the company does production work for those agencies' clients. But as the world of marketing evolved, clients began to ask Radical to work with them directly. That presented a challenge. Radical wanted to do the best work for both sides, but it didn't want to step on anyone's toes.

At the same time, Radical provides a home for quite a few directors, and the company must feed and support the directors' careers and protect their reputations. So in different situations Radical juggles the roles of talent manager, agency, and content-production company—and oftentimes the priority of one is not the priority of the others. Radical's integrity puts its partners at ease and reassures them that the company's goal is creating the best work, as opposed to squeezing out the most profit. This value also acts as a guide in choosing like-minded clients, partners, and employees and ensures that Radical doesn't find itself in compromising positions down the road.

While many production companies have come and gone over the decades, Radical has been consistently successful. That said, integrity must forever be nurtured inside the organization, because it would vanish in an instant if the company succumbed to the lure of the quick buck.

While the culture of some companies urges employees to prioritize profits, the people of Radical are encouraged to prioritize high-quality work and fairness to all parties. As the core value driving the culture, integrity colors behavior and decisions, and its absence would be quickly noticed. As an example, Jon shares a story about a tricky situation that arose during the shooting of a commercial:

> *A significant director went off the rails on an agency creative person for a ridiculous reason, and I removed him from the project in the best interest of the agency and its client. No one could believe I would do such a thing—especially the director. But we had worked for these folks for so*

many years, and I explained to the founder of the agency, "You deserve better. We can't risk our relationship with you or your longtime relationship with your client." We replaced the director with another talent who graciously accepted the responsibility. The new guy worked hard at turning things around, collaborated beautifully with the previously bruised creative team, and the campaign went on to win a Titanium* at the Cannes Lions Festival.

Jon believes that when values are strong, the culture feeds itself. Great work strengthens the culture, and a strong culture produces more great work.

Radical has about 150 people on staff, but the nature of producing content is such that it employs thousands of freelancers in any given year. Jon notes that those people appreciate Radical's strong culture as well.

We're often thanked by freelance people for what makes Radical different. I'm always curious when I hear that. Are we really that different? They might not use the word "integrity," but they talk about honesty and commitment, the loyalty and attitude of our employees, and the way we treat people. It comes back to us in spades in the most positive way. Whether they're staff or freelance, they consider themselves family.

Reputation is a major factor in attracting new business, and Radical's behaviors and accomplishments serve to enhance its reputation for integrity. The company has turned a positive human value into a defining part of its business.

But can't any RadicalMedia competitor claim to embrace the same value? Of course it can. However, claims are cheap. To effectively drive a company's business, values must run deep. Imitating isn't the same as believing.

---

* The Titanium Lion is a special award at the Cannes Lions Festival given to "breakthrough ideas which are provocative and point to a new direction in the industry."

Values Can't Be Copied

While in Seoul, South Korea, I met with Ted Chung, who at the time was CEO of credit card company Hyundai Card, as well as Hyundai Capital and Hyundai Commercial. These three companies are the financial arms of parent company Hyundai Motor Group. They were created to help consumers and businesses finance vehicles and to provide other financial and business services.

Ted is a business celebrity in South Korea, largely due to the remarkable transformation he orchestrated at Hyundai Card. As a result of his success, in 2015 he was elevated to the position of vice chairman at all three companies.

When he accepted the job in 2003, Hyundai Card and Hyundai Capital together were losing $765 million per year. Ten years later, under Ted's leadership, they were looking at a profit of $910 million per year. Key to this turnaround were the major changes Ted introduced at Hyundai Card.

He started by instilling a new set of values in the company. One of these values was the love of design. This has not only helped drive Hyundai Card's reversal of fortunes but also inspired the workforce, transformed the company's physical space, and presented an aspirational image to customers. It's also contributed to the company's new sense of simplicity, acting as a guideline for many decisions.

Hyundai Card treats its credit cards as if they were jewels. Not only do the cards have an artistic, minimalist design, but they are delivered to customers in elegant packaging. This focus on design encourages customers to see the company's offerings as premium products, reflective of a premium lifestyle. (Ted actually designed the first card that launched upon his arrival at the company, tinkering at home with logos, layout, and colors.)

Ted believes that for design to have a true impact on the way the company does business, it must be a visible part of the culture. He's created a physical work space in which that influence is clearly felt.

When I visited Hyundai Card, I was expecting to see the headquarters of a financial company, with all the restrained imagery that evokes. Instead what I found was part design studio, part museum, and part technology showcase.

The lobby is simple and elegant, greeting visitors with a display of media art by British artist Julian Opie. The Design Lab was designed by French architect Jean Nouvel. The design library was jaw-dropping—bigger than that of any ad agency I have ever worked with and even bigger than the library inside Apple's secret design studios. Café M, used by employees and visitors, is also beautifully designed, including chairs conceived by the lauded Danish designer Verner Panton.

I asked Ted if he was concerned that his competitors would try to gain ground by copying Hyundai Card's values or the ways in which they are communicated. He wasn't concerned.

> *They are already trying to copy us—but they don't have our DNA. So they don't really understand what we are doing. I could probably open up my entire business plan to them and it wouldn't really matter. They've hired designers and marketers, and in some cases they've even hired people away from Hyundai Card. But if you don't have the DNA and you don't have the vision, copying another company is pointless.*

By creating aspirational products, the company has cultivated an aura of coolness—and Ted stresses that coolness is not a superficial thing. It's actually a reflection of the company's beliefs.

> *When Steve Jobs showed the first iPhone, it was cool because of its design and functionality—but also because Steve Jobs and Apple had earned respect for their values and all they'd accomplished. Another company could copy the iPhone and create a good product, but that alone wouldn't make it cool.*

Coolness, says Ted, is born of a company's values. When those values align with customers' values, a deeper connection results. Values become both an attraction and a reward.

Ted tells the story of a trip he took to New York City, during which he stopped in to see a showcase store that had just been opened by a major consumer electronics company. He was struck by the store, but not in a positive way. The store was "cool," but it felt generic and didn't project the company's values. It failed miserably in conveying the "why" behind the company's products.

In contrast, Ted clearly sees Apple's values in its retail stores. They're the same values he sees elsewhere in the Apple world—online, in packaging, in advertising, and in the products themselves. At every opportunity Apple reinforces its values of simplicity, design, quality, and enhancing people's lives. In Ted's thinking, Apple succeeds because those values are authentic to the brand. Without authenticity, "cool" means little.

Down in Sydney, CEO John McGrath of the real estate company McGrath Limited also sees his company's culture as something that can't be co-opted by competitors. He sees culture as a powerful recruiting tool. Still, he doesn't go out of his way to drill culture into people. In John's view culture is caught, not taught.

The culture is something people pick up when they're part of the business. You can tell them about it up front, and you can give them some information about what their experience will be. But it's their actual experience that forms their perceptions.

John puts his energy into ensuring that people truly experience the culture from the start. He brings people in from the branches to spend time in the head office. Everyone gets a "starting day," in which they begin to absorb the culture—not by formal instruction but by interacting with their new colleagues. Everyone, from the junior assistant in the farthest office to a new general manager, is required to experience that first day in the business. John goes out of his way to attend every starting-day session so he can introduce himself and share his feelings about what makes the company unique.

John believes culture inspires people to perform. What people see should prove that those who work there love what they do; that they want to be the best; and that they're committed to excellence. Further, he says it's okay if some people just don't fit into the company's culture,

> *It doesn't appeal to everyone, to be very honest—and that's part of the attraction. People know when they join us that the most important thing here is integrity, which in our industry is almost negligible. So I say to people, "This is either going to be heaven or hell."*

If a culture is strong, the standard for performance is unmistakable. That offers instant appeal to most newcomers—and makes a few realize quickly that they're not in the right place.

> *You come to McGrath if you're committed to excellence, if you love serving clients, if you're passionate about what you do, and if you tell the truth 24/7. If any of those four boxes are not ticked, you really need to go now. We're black and white about that. It's part of the recruitment process. It's no good bringing someone on only to hear him say, "Oh, damn, that's not what I was signing up for."*

Like that of Hyundai Card in South Korea, the nature of McGrath's culture is well known even though the company's values are not plastered on the walls of the workplace. The principles are communicated by the experience of working there.

Some companies, however, find it effective to formalize their values and actively instill them in the organization by various means.

Values Can Be Carved in Stone

The Container Store has achieved retail success that almost defies believability. Its first store opened in 1978, and since that time the company has grown at least 20 percent every year. It has also made *Fortune*'s "100 Best Places to Work" list for fifteen consecutive years—perhaps the first clue that The Container Store has a particularly good culture.

I talked to CEO Kip Tindell at length about his company's values and how he continuously reinforces them. At the company's founding Kip authored what he calls the Foundation Principles. There are seven of them. (If you're looking for something profound about the number seven, don't. Kip figured that since most people can't even remember all of the Ten Commandments, he'd make it easier and go with seven. Simplicity strikes again.)

The Foundation Principles address a number of values, including communication, treating the store's vendors well, developing intuition, maintaining the air of excitement, and exceeding customers' expectations. For Kip these principles perfectly explain his company's success.

> *In our hiring we go through the Foundation Principles. In our training we go through the Foundation Principles. It is the skeletal framework of our culture. It is the reason we do what we do.*

These principles are the core of The Container Store's simplicity. They eliminate the need for the complicated rules and procedures often found in companies of similar size. The Foundation Principles are also empowering, in that they give employees the freedom to work in their own individual way, without supervisors constantly looking over their shoulder.

> *We're not smart enough to tell thousands of employees what to do in a given situation. We can't tell thousands of employees how to answer the phone. We don't even attempt to do that. What we do is get people to agree on these very simple ends. Then we liberate them to choose the means to those ends, so they can provide the best customer service, the best solution, and the greatest value. We unshackle them to use their own creative genius.*

There's no question in Kip's mind that the principles have led the company to higher productivity, as well as happier customers, employees, and vendors.

The danger in many companies is that guidelines like these tend to be seen and noted but don't have much impact on the company's day-to-day business. That's not the case at The Container Store, because these principles truly are the company's foundation.

You can go into one of our stores and ask people, "Do the Foundation Principles really guide all your business actions?" I think you'll find that the answer is yes. They aren't just words on the wall. Our people are constantly talking about them. Having these principles is much better than having a bossy boss tell you what to do.

The Foundation Principles are frequently celebrated in meetings and internal communications, which encourages people to do their jobs within these guidelines. Because the company's values are clearly articulated and regularly reinforced, the culture is continually strengthened. The values inspire employees to support one another as they strive to provide the thing that sets them apart—amazing customer service.

The pursuit of exceptional service was also essential to building a winning culture at discount broker Charles Schwab. Schwab's culture was also formalized as a set of values and heavily socialized throughout the company. The company's "product" was actually a better financial future, and providing the best service was essential to making customers comfortable and earning their trust.

Schwab's former CEO Dave Pottruck helped guide the company through a period of dramatic growth in the late 1990s. A strong culture was a major driver of the company's expansion, says Dave, and that culture was built purposefully and methodically.

It was in the early part of the 1990s that we got really focused on our culture. I hired Terry Pearce, a leadership communications coach, to help with my leadership skills and my speeches, and just thinking about how I act as a leader of the company along with Chuck [founder Charles Schwab]. Terry was very focused on culture, and he helped me understand that culture was something that needed care and attention.

Dave's feeling is that companies will always have a culture, and that culture will develop with or without you. So you have to think about what culture you want to have and what you might be able to do to shape it.

Culture to me is incredibly important because it ties to the mission and values. That's what culture really is. It is the mission and values, and the behaviors that make them real.

How do you want people to act every day? What is true north? Do people have to turn to a manual before they can make a decision? Or do they know how to do the right thing by customers because the values are so well understood?

As Schwab's leader, Dave devoted a major chunk of his time to talking about the culture, investing in it, and reinforcing it. He put together an off-site meeting with the top hundred people in the company with the purpose of crafting a mission statement that would help shape the culture.

It took all weekend to do. The more they talked about it, Schwab's values boiled down to six things that these leaders wanted the company to be and every employee to understand.

These six values guided every policy in our company and every decision. Just six values. These values were fairness, empathy, responsiveness, striving, teamwork, and trustworthiness.

If you asked any of our thousands of employees about the Schwab values, they'd know them well. These were the values that guided their decisions every day. As long as they acted on these values, they'd be acting in the best interest of the company and its customers.

What makes employees happiest and most fulfilled is when their personal values align with the company's values. If there is a significant gap between those values, says Dave, people aren't going to be happy in their work. Without that level of personal satisfaction, they won't do the job you want them to do.

Dave and his team made things easier for all when they drilled down to the six values that defined service at Schwab. Now they had something they could share throughout the organization, and something that would help them attract employees who aspired to the same values.

One good measure of a company's culture is how long people stick around. I've been associated with some ad agencies and clients where quite a few people have been there ten years, fifteen years, or even longer. That's natural when a company and its employees are aligned in their values, as they were at Schwab. Dave elaborates:

> *We had very low turnover at Schwab. Very low. In fact, in my entire time at Schwab, spanning twenty years, we had at one point hundreds of senior vice presidents, and only one ever left to take a job in the financial-services industry—and that was to become CEO of a start-up.*
>
> *There were people who got rich and quit. There were people we had to ask to leave because their jobs outgrew them. But no one ever left to go work for a competitor. Ever. We never lost anyone to a competitor.*

That's the power of a strong corporate culture. It keeps like-minded people fulfilled, motivated, and committed to the mission as one.

A Culture of Commitment

When you walk into Whole Foods Market, you might not think it's the simplest of stores. It's a big place with thousands of food items. What does strike you is the company's ability to provide fresh, healthful, natural food in every aisle and on every shelf. The company has created a culture fueled by a devotion to healthier living.

The strong culture of Whole Foods serves to simplify decisions and choices at every level. It attracts employees who share the passion and it unites the workforce in a common purpose. It also creates the in-store experience that resonates so strongly with customers.

What started in 1980 with one store and a staff of nineteen has grown into a network of four hundred stores with over $15 billion in annual sales.

Though Whole Foods faced hardships in 2015 due to financial and competitive pressures, the company's growth since inception has been phenomenal. What started in 1980 with one store and a staff of nineteen has evolved into a network of four hundred stores with over $15 billion in annual sales.

Co-CEO Walter Robb attributes the company's success to a clear mission that forms a foundation for the culture and delights customers.

> *There is an elegant clarity to what we do. We carry nothing with artificial flavors, colors, or ingredients. Nothing, nothing, nothing. There are no exceptions to that rule—or any of the standards for the products in our store. There is perfect clarity on that line in the sand.*
>
> *There's a kernel of simplicity—a kernel of truth—for Whole Foods. That is, when you walk in the store, you just feel good. You feel the energy. And that's different from what you feel in other supermarkets.*

Over the years, some analysts have advised Whole Foods to grow further by broadening its food selection (read: loosen standards). But the company doesn't stray from its pledge to sell only food that's good for people and for the world. "Pure ingredients most of the time" just won't cut it. "No" is an easy answer when your values are strong.

To understand Whole Foods' success and the importance of its culture, it helps to understand its roots.

The quest for more healthful food began in the early 1970s with a generation that believed food had become too processed and too far removed from its natural state. Supermarkets were selling white flour, white sugar, white rice, and a great many frozen foods. As Walter's generation matured, a movement began to take back the land, so to speak. People became interested in grinding their own grain, making their own bread, growing their own vegetables, and so on.

At its birth Whole Foods was really just trying to plant the idea that more healthful food mattered. It was trying to communicate that "whole" foods—with a small *w*—provide greater health to individuals, communities, and the planet. It's an idea that resonates even more today, when people are taking more responsibility for their health in their diet and lifestyle.

Still, it's a huge leap from "It's a good idea" to "It's a good business." Walter credits the business success of Whole Foods to its ability to build a culture around this simple mission—one that motivates employees, creating a feeling of participation and fulfillment.

One of our greatest strengths is our culture. I define "culture" as the mission as practiced over time. It's a living, breathing thing. All great companies have a culture. It's not something you can copy—you have to create your own organically. And then you have to keep investing in it as you grow.

Whole Foods has a strong sense of purpose or mission, but the culture is really built upon empowerment, collaboration, and innovation. Our first two core values are to satisfy and delight the customer and to create team member happiness. We often talk about team member happiness and customer happiness in the same breath. Because if we look after the team members, they'll look after the customers. Those two are inextricably linked.

We all know what a pleasure it is to shop in a place where knowledgeable salespeople are genuinely eager to help. This is the behavior of employees who are respected and empowered by their companies, and this is the experience that creates loyal customers.

To instill this behavior in its employees, Whole Foods has built a culture where the workforce feels they're not just part of the company—they're part of the mission. That's an important distinction.

There's a two-way dialogue between management and employees and an emphasis on transparency of information. Full-time staff vote on benefits every year. Employees participate in the savings they create through sales-building efforts or more efficient scheduling. There are regular town halls where people are free to speak. There are panel interviews for new hires, and the people on the panel are usually those who are affected by the hiring decision. Walter says it's all about empowerment and collaboration, with the simple mission of the company at the center of it all.

> *Whole Foods is very much a distributed intelligence culture. We hoped that by creating this petri dish of empowerment, things would continue to unfold, and that's exactly what's happened. I think most people today want to work for something that's bigger than a paycheck. They want to feel like they're making a difference in people's lives—including their own.*

In some companies values are codified, but unless they are effectively celebrated (as they are at The Container Store and Charles Schwab), they may be relegated to the role of mere decorations on the cafeteria bulletin board. Not the case at Whole Foods. The values are "alive," says Walter, because they are constantly being talked about. People can see that they're real, because management decisions are aligned with those values.

> *There is power in the simplicity of leading with mission, values, and culture. I believe there's a next-level simplicity around using those things as your organizing principles in business and really sticking to it. There's a power and clarity to that, which Whole Foods has.*

For most leaders building a culture is a challenge, but at least they can focus on a single culture. Some, however, don't have the luxury of "oneness." For them, building a culture requires a special effort.

Culture Unites a Company

Imagine trying to create a unified culture when the company is actually a collection of unique cultures. Video game maker Electronic Arts faces the challenge of bringing together a number of disparate constituencies.

COO Bryan Neider explains that because today's games are a marriage of technology and entertainment, EA must bring engineers and artists together, even though these two groups don't normally gravitate toward each other. The company relies on its culture to encourage interactions between the two, creating synergy.

Adding to the challenge is the fact that EA brings in a number of groups through acquisitions, says Bryan, and these groups typically arrive with their own distinct cultures.

> *The sports guys are very different from the teams that make Battlefield and Sims. We can generalize about commonality, but the issues and problems they solve are unique for each game. Keeping it simple becomes a huge, huge job.*

It takes effort, but in the end it's a question of providing support for the company's overall values while respecting the values that exist within individual groups.

> *We try to get the culture of EA to permeate all. We try to find these common threads, then reward and celebrate great entertainment.*

The goal is to create a feeling of being on the same team with the same vision, even though the reality is that multiple teams are creating unique game experiences. In practice, many companies face a cultural challenge similar to that of EA. They consist of different departments or physical locations that have little interaction with one another.

In such companies a strong culture is the glue that creates the feeling of "we."

Culture Is the Fuel for the Mission

The mission is what propels a company forward. But a clear mission does not guarantee success any more than a solid foundation guarantees a beautiful home.

For the mission to have meaning, it must be activated, communicated, and embraced by the workforce. That's why culture is so important. It's the fuel that transforms the mission from concept to reality.

A powerful culture reflects and promotes the company's values. It empowers people to contribute to companywide goals even as they act independently. It unifies the workforce and functions as a shield against complexity.

The bad news: There are more companies in this world with cultures of complexity than with cultures of simplicity. Complicated companies have their defenses built in, and they often reject those who try to bring change.

The good news: Complexity is not a permanent condition. Cultures can and do change, even if the task seems nearly impossible. The key is momentum. The more you do to create a culture of simplicity, the easier it gets.

Chapter 3
Simplicity Loves a Leader

Maybe it's because simplicity looks easier than it is, or because the path to simplicity often seems obvious. But the fact is, many companies behave as if simplicity will happen all by itself.

It rarely does. Without a champion, simplicity is no match for the forces of complexity that are forever nipping at its heels. Fortunately, champions of simplicity do exist.

They're the business leaders who view every part of their business through the lens of simplicity and find ways to make their companies more nimble, more responsive, more effective, more competitive, and more important.

They do it all with that unique combination of brains and common sense. They're experts in their industry, but they're also human beings with a firm grasp of what makes people act as they do.

That said, leaders have their individual styles, and the methods by which they bring simplicity into their companies can vary. Some are top-down managers, some are more collaborative, and some are a combination thereof. In this chapter we'll take a look at the philosophies, behaviors, and personalities that have enabled a growing number of leaders to guide their organizations to a simpler place.

Leaders Who Empower, Not Dominate

Having led the Apple Store effort from its inception through eleven years of success, Ron Johnson logged countless hours of quality time with Steve Jobs. Ron observed that Steve had certain traits that automatically put him on a different plane from many business leaders.

First and foremost, Steve knew things—and he also knew that he didn't know everything. Having grown up in the industry, he gained the strength of experience at a very young age. But for any challenge he had to face, and for whatever advice he might need, all he had to do was pick up the phone. He could tap the brains of the smartest people on earth. Says Ron:

> When Steve wanted to get into retail, he could talk to Mickey Drexler.* If he wanted to talk to a world-class architect, he could call a leader at LVMH.† If someone said Steve Jobs was on the line, who wouldn't take the call? Steve had incredible impact and influence, along with the wisdom that can only be gained over time.
>
> Few people have this advantage. Bill Gates had it. Some of today's other young leaders will have it. But it's rare to find that kind of experience in someone so young.

Of course, every public company has a board of directors, and the purpose of a board is to provide the company with sage advice from experts across a range of disciplines. But Steve's ability to reach out to just about anyone on the planet proved to be a tremendous advantage in the innovation business.

---

* Chairman and CEO of J.Crew and former CEO of Gap.

† A unique company comprising seventy "houses," each creating high-quality products in major sectors of the luxury market.

The depth of Steve's experience also helped him understand the limits of his own capabilities.

I think Steve learned over time that he had to surround himself with people who could help create the culture he desired, because he didn't necessarily have the day-to-day skills to do it himself.

Former Apple marketing leader Steve Wilhite focuses on another trait that made Jobs such an effective leader: He was able to guide the company from a high-altitude perspective one moment and dive deep into tiny details the next. Says Wilhite:

It wasn't that he was micromanaging. He was showing a genuine level of interest. I've worked with iconic and amazing CEOs, but never with anyone who had Steve's breadth of curiosity and inquisitiveness and the enthusiasm for fine detail in virtually every aspect of what we were doing.

Agreed. In my own experience working with Jobs, I never felt micromanaged, nor did our marketing team. We felt we had the attention of a CEO who was eager to share ideas and opinions, and one who was also capable of being swayed by someone else's passionate argument.

What amazed Wilhite most was Jobs's eagerness to participate, even though it seemed that he couldn't possibly have the time to participate to the degree that he did. Jobs would spend days and nights with Jony Ive in the design studio working on the physical curves of a product or the tactile quality of a button, things that few CEOs would likely get involved with. Again, he wasn't dictating to Jony. He was simply eager to participate in debate and development. Ensuring perfection in every detail was part of Jobs's passion, Wilhite recalls.

Working with Steve was not an easy task, but it was inspiring. His band-width, his ability to grasp different concepts, his passion for delivering an off-the-charts experience—I've never experienced anything like that with any other CEO.

This is also consistent with my experience. I often cite stories about times our agency would be preparing print ads and TV commercials. Never once did Steve order me or anyone else at the agency to do one thing or another, creatively speaking. What he loved to do was express opinions and engage in debate, and those discussions often resulted in a better ad. As the ultimate decision maker, he simply wanted to be involved in the process. Having Steve involved was infinitely simpler than the alternative—working with levels of approvals and opinions from people who might not have the skills to appreciate the big picture.

Email was Steve's preferred method of staying involved from a distance. His response time, often a matter of minutes, was a constant source of amazement given the number of emails he must have received every day. And he insisted on handling emails himself, rather than allowing an assistant to judge what was important enough for his attention.

He wouldn't reply to everyone, but he had a system of sorts. If he felt a customer email merited a response, he would jot off a quick reply. If he spotted a good idea, he might forward the note to the appropriate person in his world, inside or outside of Apple. (The lawyers beseeched him never to look at unsolicited ideas, in order to avoid legal complications—with only limited success.) I would sometimes receive forwarded emails from Steve on the topic of advertising, along with a note to the effect of "What do you think of this?" Or, in the case of someone pointing out that *Think different* was grammatically incorrect, he might say, "Please respond to this person." He didn't expect a follow-up. He just expected it to get done.

Communication, especially the way Steve handled it, is as empowering as it is clarifying—which is why it's such a helpful tool in the cause of simplification.

That said, leaders who believe in simplicity understand that supporting simplicity is only part of the battle. Leading the charge in defending against complexity is every bit as important.

Serving as Chief Uncomplicator

As CEO of his Sydney-based real estate network, John McGrath believes that it's his responsibility to both remove and resist complexity.

One way he succeeds is by filtering complexity from his business plans. He insists that every business plan be distilled to its essence, written as concisely as humanly possible.

> *I don't like any more than a page. It's all about pulling back to the essential bits. The manifestation of simplicity is removing the layers of complexity, the excuses, and all the unnecessary and unproductive debate.*
>
> *Complexity is easy. Simplicity is harder. The most effective way to present real estate to prospective buyers is to refine it down to the information that's most important.*

John cites Apple's example when he talks about distilling information, quoting Steve Jobs about the importance of "peeling away the layers of the onion" to get at something pure and simple.

In John's thinking, simplicity can come from many different places— one of which is a leader's personal preparation. Remaining healthy and keeping his mind uncluttered has a direct impact on his business, so he keeps a rigid schedule. He's up at five o'clock every morning and starts his day by going to the gym. One thing he does *not* do is listen to or watch the news.

> *Thirty minutes of the news is thirty minutes of negative thoughts. I haven't watched the news for five years. This is my simplicity—removing things that are negative. I put thirty minutes' worth of positive podcasts into my brain rather than thirty minutes of negative world news.*

John prefers to spend his time thinking about positive things he can do for the company, like chasing clients, recruiting brilliant staff, coaching the team, and holding the company to high standards.

He also embraces the power of routine. He once thought routine was a killer of creativity and spontaneity but has come to believe the saying that "routine sets you free." By creating a weekly schedule that sets aside regular times for group meetings, one-on-one meetings, client meetings, etc., John ensures that he has the personal time and space to think about innovation within McGrath.

As chief uncomplicator, John sets the standards and makes the final decisions. Still, most decisions are open to debate, which puts ideas to the test before they're implemented. Since he makes hiring quality people such a high priority, he thinks it would be crazy not to give these people an active role in guiding the company. He's open to being swayed by a good argument. He gets that there will always be some level of "He's the boss" going on during a discussion, which can be intimidating to some—but that actually filters out those who aren't passionate about their opinions, he says.

> *My style is extremely direct, which people who don't know me might occasionally misplace as being an ass. My team knows me, and they know that my intention is to get the best result for them as quickly as possible. Let's just cut to the chase and deal with the issues.*

Meetings at McGrath tend to be punchy and short. John may cut someone off if they start to ramble, but everyone gets that he's not out to bruise anyone's ego. In fact, he wants his staff to understand that he really does care about their personal success and happiness.

> *I'm interested in you. You're not just a number in my budget. You're a real human being with a pulse, and fears, and excitement. As long as you know I care and you understand where I come from, that I want all of us to succeed—we can concentrate on the work.*

Of course, one of the perks of being the founder is that you've got leeway to be meaner or moodier. But, in John's words, a smart and good founder understands that he's not there to belittle people—he's there to lift them up. He's willing to accept mistakes, provided that those mistakes result from thinking bigger or more creatively. What a leader of simplicity cannot tolerate is mistakes born of a lack of attention to detail.

I was curious to know if there was any kind of "fear factor" at McGrath, people feeling the pressure to perform or risk getting sacked. I asked because in my ad agency experience, we in the creative group would often discuss the pros and cons of leaders who were warm and approachable as opposed to those who were cold, results-oriented, and quick to fire if necessary. People not mentally prepared to handle the pressure from the colder type would suffer anxiety that only made matters worse.

John doesn't believe in creating fear, but he does believe in creating clarity.

> *I don't think we have a fear factor. But there is absolute clarity that we only accept great work, and that we don't want to hear excuses for non-delivery of results or quality of work—so you'd better get it right or there is going to be a problem.*

While day-to-day work is important, John sees the leader's job as being more concerned about the company's direction, how it's innovating and keeping abreast of what's happening in other industries in other parts of the world.

He references Tim Cook, who often speaks of Apple's discipline and how the company says no to intriguing ideas every day. That's the kind of enterprise John wants to run. He wants to innovate, but very selectively. It's every bit as important to execute perfectly on the things that are known to work beautifully.

> *We have to say no to many ideas, choose only the best ideas, and then execute brilliantly. Apple has only a small number of products—but those few products have made it the best business on the planet.*

Looking at the way John runs his company, one would have to say McGrath is a "leader-driven collaboration." John has confidence in the decisions of his executive team, but to keep things simple he has his hand firmly on the helm.

Over at The Container Store, CEO Kip Tindell also believes that keeping things simple is a group effort.

Communication, Collaboration, and Simplification

When he built The Container Store, Kip was determined to avoid the problems he'd observed elsewhere, where barriers form between management and the workforce, and employees don't feel empowered. Instead, Kip says that his leadership style places a high priority on communication—and not just in the traditional sense of the word.

We communicate all around, up, down, and sideways. There's no rigid hierarchy where this person reports to that person, so I need to go through one person with everything. That is so unproductive.

A rigid structure creates the air of formality that exists in so many companies, and that type of atmosphere would work against The Container Store's mission, culture, and values. Enforced hierarchies, in Kip's view, are the by-product of a different mentality.

Guys went off to World War II—many came back and started businesses, and they felt that the militaristic approach was the proper way to do that. That may be a good way to run the military, but it's a terrible way to run a business.

You can get a good sense of a company's culture by the way it structures meetings and the frequency with which it holds those meetings. It's probably no surprise that the leaders in this book, fans of simplicity all, prefer a more casual work environment. "Less meeting, more doing" is a common theme.

As the leader, Kip offers only one rule for meetings at The Container Store: Use time efficiently. Having a meeting agenda is a good idea, and those who attend a meeting are expected to contribute.

What's missing from his style of leadership is the intimidation factor. Kip has tried to create an atmosphere where people feel safe sharing new ideas and believe their thoughts are valued.

I don't want to be too important to the business or have the top executives be too important to the business.

I think it's handy to have leaders who are also founders—but then they need to step back and make sure it's not all about them. Some of my favorite companies have leaders who have allowed their incredibly talented people to take ownership of ideas.

The work environment at The Container Store is highly collaborative, and the proof that this environment fosters success is there for everyone to see.

We started a little business with $35,000 and now it's worth about $2 billion. Not all of this is kumbaya. But it works a lot better than the other way of doing business.

One big reason Kip is so keen on collaboration is that cross-pollination of ideas yields interesting and compelling results. When he gets the vice presidents together to problem-solve, create, or innovate, he's using "the whole brain." Each individual has a terrific yet different perspective on the company, and together, says Kip, these perspectives and talents add up to something more.

Collaboration creates appreciation, love, and a pride for the organization. You're working with a lot of great people, and you're exposed to their thinking. Collaborative groups are multiculturalism—the diversity of the company at work.

The danger, as many have experienced, is that collaboration can lead to chaos born of too many opinions and agendas, or strategies that emerge from compromise. However, Kip sees collaboration as a simplifying force. He leads a large company that requires people with different skills. Collaboration creates opportunities for these people to benefit from one another's expertise and go forward with a single focus.

At The Container Store collaboration does not disintegrate into complexity. That's because team members have strong shared values and they have a mission-driven leader who participates in the process.

Andrew Bassat, cofounder and CEO of SEEK, an online job-listings company based in Melbourne, Australia, has a similar view about the power of collaboration.

Andrew and his brother Paul started the company in 1997, when they realized that "this Internet thing" could revolutionize the traditional system of job hunting, which seemed to be stuck in the age of classified ads.

With Andrew's collaborative style of leadership, SEEK has grown to become the major online jobs resource in Australia and beyond. It is now a $4 billion company with operations in New Zealand, China, Southeast Asia, Brazil, and Mexico. All together, its websites log 275 million visits per month. Andrew's success as a leader earned him the title of 2013 Australian Entrepreneur of the Year from Ernst & Young.

Andrew meets frequently with his management team, improving ideas by going through iteration after iteration. Debate is encouraged, with the goal of getting everyone on the same page. He explains:

It's a good process. There are no sacred cows in terms of the conversation. No one feels that I'm giving them edicts they can't question, or vice versa. We try to poke holes in each other's strategies. We have a good back-and-forth. You've got a problem with it, you say why and you ask the questions.

If someone doesn't have good answers to my questions, they'll need to change their view or come back with better answers. And that works in both directions.

By the time the group arrives at a decision, it is no longer just one person's idea. The team has passionately and vigorously challenged the decision, debate has concluded, and it is now owned by the group. It's an open process that allows all participants to appreciate the reasons behind a decision.

As is always the case in honest debate, the decibel level in the room can rise. Though some might take criticism personally and get defensive or even get angry, the team supports the process—and it's been instrumental to the company's success. Andrew observes that those who believe their wisdom makes collaboration unnecessary are often the ones who make mistakes.

When it comes to projects initiated within the company, Andrew's policy is derived from common sense.

If it's something I need to be involved in, I encourage people to give me their early thoughts. Don't spend three months working on it with a whole big team and then bring the finished product to me. Show me the concept, we decide, "Yes, this fits," then go and take care of the details.

Early involvement of the leader is one of the most sacred principles of simplicity. Asking teams to work for weeks or months before the decision maker gets involved is a recipe for frustration (and wasted effort). Yet so many companies work exactly that way.

Just a few words from the leader to kick off the project, or some feedback at checkpoints along the way, can be invaluable to the team. For the leader it's another opportunity to interact personally, reinforcing values and pollinating different groups within the company. The challenge becomes simpler when people hear the leader's thinking firsthand.

SEEK is hardly a small company by most measures. Still, it's easy to argue that bigger organizations face bigger challenges in finding ways to simplify.

Bigger, yes. Insurmountable, no.

When Tech Giants Simplify—or Not

In *Insanely Simple* I was critical of Intel for making its marketing effort far more complicated than necessary. My time as Intel's ad agency creative director came immediately after my *Think different* years at Apple's agency, and the transition was jarring to say the least. I endured endless meetings, endless research, endless revisions, and had to deal with a multitude of approvers—all of which did more harm than good.

In my head I couldn't help but compare Intel's way with Apple's far simpler way, which emphasized ideas over process, an absence of hierarchy, and direct involvement with the ultimate decision maker. In the years since I was involved in Intel's marketing, the company has demonstrated a unique ability to simultaneously lead for simplicity and undermine its own effort to do so.

On the positive side, it empowered a VP of marketing, who streamlined the processes by which marketing campaigns were developed and forged a positive and productive partnership with Intel's lead advertising agency. Over a period of several years the higher quality of Intel advertising became evident. Instead of relying on odd characters such as animated aliens and dancing clean-suit workers as they had in the past, the ads told more human stories about advanced technology that was born at Intel. They even strayed from the audio pneumonic (the Intel "bong") that had been heard at the end of the company's commercials for decades, instead using a chorus of real people. The company was actually showing some charm as it claimed technology leadership.

Then, in 2013, Brian Krzanich took over the role of CEO. With a mandate for change, Krzanich pressed the company to reduce complexity and shorten time lines. One concept he promoted was radically different for Intel: "Fast beats perfect."

The old Intel took way too much time examining options, testing, tweaking, and then testing and tweaking again. Rethinking this process would allow Intel to create and respond at the pace demanded by the tech industry.

Krzanich urged employees to appreciate the difference between *speed* and *velocity*. In his thinking, speed means going fast, while velocity means moving quickly toward a specific target. Intel, he said, needed to focus on the latter. Management would identify where the company needed to go and then move toward that goal quickly and aggressively. The push for velocity inspired the company to streamline processes, enabling it to shorten traditional time lines for product development.

That was all positive. When it came to the marketing effort, however, Krzanich did not lead for simplicity. In fact, he fell into a behavior that's all too common in big companies. As part of his overall shake-up, he replaced the VP of advertising with his own person.

Unfortunately, most executives appointed as part of a shake-up feel compelled to shake things up, whether or not the department deserves shaking. And so key marketing people were suddenly gone, and the newly configured group had to basically reinvent the wheel. Not the simplest way to work.

The result was that Intel, as a marketer, reverted to its big-company form, creating advertising homogenized by research. For many years leading up to the publishing of this book, Intel's advertising has hovered between invisible and unremarkable.

IBM is another technology giant that grapples with speed and complexity. Its computing products are by nature complex, yet in 2005, with one move, IBM undertook one of the most dramatic acts of simplification in business history.

To focus IBM on its strengths and eliminate products that were draining company resources without significant ROI, then-CEO Lou Gerstner shed the entire IBM personal computer division. This was a shocker, as IBM had been a driving force behind the business PC revolution years earlier.

But times had changed. PC profits had declined dramatically as new PC companies emerged and value manufacturers relentlessly drove prices lower.

Gerstner had the audacity to lead for simplicity. He decided that IBM would be better served by selling off its PC business and putting all of its resources into enterprise services. As a result, IBM profited greatly for many years, though it ran into tough times more recently due to a mix of questionable financial strategies.

I spoke about leadership styles with Steve Mills, who is executive vice president of IBM Software and Systems. He's responsible for 100,000 employees around the world who power IBM's $40 billion software business.

Steve started by stating the obvious: IBM is not Apple. Whereas Apple has historically been driven by a single personality, IBM's culture is very different. It operates in team mode, not individual mode. Still, leadership is important for making decisions and moving the organization forward. He talked about leading within IBM.

There is an element of personality and force of will that powers the organization along. And that's important. Decisions have to be made, so you have to be willing to make them.

Since IBM cannot afford to stand still, Steve echoes the sentiment of Intel's Brian Krzanich, saying that speed is sometimes of greater benefit than perfection. IBM Software and Systems spends more than $6 billion annually on R&D, and the software Steve develops is designed to meet challenges of global proportions. For him it's actually more about embracing complexity and delivering solutions on time than about selling simplicity.

We're geared toward solving very sophisticated, high-performance computing transaction processing. We support the transaction systems that run the world today. Whether it's banking, financial systems, exchanges, credit card companies, insurance companies, airline reservations, shipping companies—the list goes on and on. We don't shy away from complexity.

But hold on—because simplicity is about to make its appearance. As soon as IBM's engineers build something that is valuable and exciting to customers, Steve directs his engineers to "make it more consumable." Which is IBM's complicated way of saying "simpler."

There is always a simpler way to design an interface, present information, put a customer at ease, and organize a workforce. Though IBM's initial solution may be complex, "making it more consumable" is what makes it more appealing to more customers over time. Even people looking for solutions to complex enterprise challenges will respond positively to elements of simplicity.

Intel and IBM are clearly not companies that radiate simplicity. Quite the opposite. They're sprawling global organizations, highly structured, and process-heavy. But even if their businesses are complex by necessity, one can see that they do benefit, sometimes in revolutionary ways, when their leaders find ways to simplify.

Later in this book we'll meet leaders from large consumer-facing companies in categories that have historically put people off with their complexity: finance and telecommunications. They've found ways to undo the complexity that had taken root over many years, and do so with eye-opening results.

But first let's take a look at a different type of company. They're not mega-corporations. They're smaller, agile, and entrepreneurial. They're already simple. How do their leaders manage to ensure that complexity doesn't take root?

Keeping the Start-up Simple as It Grows

Many of us look back at our earliest professional days and think, "Things were simpler back then." Since the statute of limitations has now expired,

I will confess that at one of my first ad agency jobs, my creative group would actually go see a movie during lunch—a very long lunch. I have no idea how we got away with that, other than the fact that things were definitely simpler then.

Similarly, a company with a thousand people spread across a network of offices might look back and remember the days when it was smaller, more agile, laser-focused, and not encumbered by layers of management and processes.

The question is, how does a leader guide a simple company so that it doesn't lose the advantages of simplicity as it becomes bigger? Success can be intoxicating—but it also opens the door to complexity.

My curiosity about the dynamics of a start-up prompted a conversation with StubHub cofounder Jeff Fluhr. Jeff had the experience of seeing his cozy start-up transform into something very, very big.

When it comes to his personal involvement with project teams, Jeff's attitude is similar to that of Andrew Bassat at SEEK. If it's a major initiative or investment, or if it requires major resources, Jeff absolutely wants to be involved as the ultimate decision maker, and he wants to be involved early. Otherwise, he's happy to let the teams take responsibility. People quickly come to realize that "this is the way we work here." That's important to Jeff, because by giving the teams more responsibility, he's building capabilities that will become more valuable as the company gets bigger.

At StubHub Jeff was gratified when he saw people working on their own. He felt that they were doing what people in a growing company should do: showing initiative.

I remember many times when something new was developed, and I got really excited about it. Thrilled with it. And it would be something that I wasn't even aware of beforehand. It was like "Wow, did the company just do that? That's pretty cool."

I have these memories of being pleasantly surprised as we grew that my team was getting things done, or putting new features in the product, or doing things with new partners. I don't ever remember anything happening that would make me wonder why they did it, or being upset that it happened.

Jeff gives people a good degree of autonomy in their decision making and tries not to have more than "a few hops" between himself and any of his people. He encourages people to make decisions on their own and consult with him only when they need him.

This is all a change of thinking from the early days of StubHub—the result of Jeff's growing older and wiser. Back then he was more of a micromanager, with his head in all the details. That was when he had unlimited bandwidth to focus on work, before he had a family.

His people started to push back on his constant presence. They said, "You're in my face, you're micromanaging me, and I don't like it." Today he's thankful that people were so honest about that, as those conversations convinced him to delegate more, giving people responsibility and autonomy. He believes this contributed to a simpler company, because it allowed people to focus on their work and cut down on unnecessary meetings. Jeff says he continues to work that way today.

I may even be a little too hands-off. But personally it's a very liberating thing, because you have good people doing stuff you don't have to do anymore. They can get a lot done, and frankly they can do it a lot better than I can in their areas of expertise. They come up with great ideas. And when you give them autonomy, they feel better about what they are doing. They feel more ownership.

Most managers would agree that it's a good idea for people to feel ownership. It's just that in companies suffering from complexity, it's more a philosophy than a reality. Jeff believes that this sense of ownership is especially important to the success of the start-up and the ability to keep the business simple. Working in this type of environment gets people excited about what they're doing. It frees them from complicated processes. It makes them more productive and happier to be part of the team.

> *I'm not saying I'm the best manager now, or that I don't sometimes micro-manage. I'm still more of an entrepreneur than a manager. But I've seen the benefits of giving people responsibility. I try to delegate as much as possible, so managers can make decisions on their own. I view myself as the ultimate arbiter of things that need to bubble up to me.*

There's no mistaking that Jeff is the final decision maker. He stays in-volved in major projects. But by empowering his managers, he's found a good way to streamline internal processes.

One thing Jeff does not tolerate is management by committee. He believes that when you have five people trying to arrive at a decision, prog-ress is painfully slow—an opinion echoed by many practitioners of simplicity.

> *At StubHub we had weekly meetings for marketing, business develop-ment, and then an executive meeting as well. These meetings were quick. I don't like to overanalyze or overruminate. That just wastes time—and time is of the essence when you're running companies in the technol-ogy space.*
>
> *You can take six months to make the perfect decision, or you can take six days to make a good decision. You may reach a perfect decision in six months, but by that time it won't be relevant. You have to make quick decisions, then act on them quickly.*

Like Intel CEO Brian Krzanich, Jeff believes in velocity—moving quickly toward a specific goal.

We've heard several champions of simplicity speak out in favor of the collaborative workplace and express their belief that it helps support a simple mission and culture. The leaders are firmly in control, but they depend on the participation of others to reach and implement important decisions.

However, a number of my interview subjects felt that top-down leadership is the most direct path to simplicity. We'll look at their practices and let you be the judge of what works best in your world.

Focus Starts at the Top

Brian Hartzer, CEO of Australia's Westpac Bank, is a big proponent of top-down management.

Westpac is literally the oldest company in Australia and its very first bank. At the end of fiscal year 2015, it was the country's second biggest bank with assets of $568 billion (in U.S. dollars), employing more than 32,000 permanent staff across 1,429 branches.

Though Brian's challenges are complex—or *because* his challenges are complex—Brian is a major believer in the power of simplicity. His office has only one bookshelf and on that shelf there are only four books. Each one is a different take on simplicity.

One of the most important ways a leader can simplify, says Brian, is to be an active participant in major projects. Echoing what we've heard from others, he expressed the belief that when the leader becomes part of the process, it simplifies in a most profound way. He relies on his teams to solve problems creatively, but his personal guidance and support has led to impressive results and improved morale. Brian explains:

> *If I were going to make one overarching observation about simplification, it's the importance of top-down direction. Because so many of us have been conditioned about collaboration and teamwork and getting people involved to win their support, many management processes that have developed—particularly in big companies—almost take as a starting point that everyone has an equal voice. It should all be collaborative. Effectively, everything is designed by committee.*

When Brian reflected on projects that have achieved the best results at Westpac, he realized that they have all been instances in which he had the opportunity to give personal direction. Ideas come from many people in his organization, but people are energized when the leader takes part. It creates focus and discourages people from trying to do too many things at once.

For example, Brian talked about home lending products, a critical part of the bank's business. Looking at the mortgage-origination process, he found that it took a number of weeks to approve a home loan. Brian pushed the team to speed up the process, believing that this would increase customer satisfaction and that would result in more sales.

At one point Brian attended a workshop with the operations and engineering teams. He learned that they were working on what they called "the one-visit mortgage." The team was quite proud of this new concept. Brian saw it differently.

> *I thought that wasn't compelling enough. I said, "Let's create the sixty-minute mortgage. You've got to figure out a way to complete the mortgage process in that period of time." The team bristled at that notion, but I felt that it had to be sixty minutes, or it just wouldn't be compelling enough.*
>
> *And then I said, "While we're at it, let's have a ten-minute top-up."*

A top-up is what you ask for when you've paid down part of your mortgage and you want to borrow additional money on that loan to finance a new expense, such as a home renovation. Oddly, this top-up process took longer than getting the original mortgage.

The team plunged into the task, and soon Westpac was offering both a sixty-minute mortgage and a ten-minute top-up—two beautifully simplified products that proved quite attractive to customers.

> *To me, one very key element of simplicity is the top-down clarity of a simple goal—and the value that gives to the teams who are trying to solve*

*the problem, to help them focus their efforts and come up with creative
solutions.*

A number of other leaders expressed similar feelings about the value of
top-down leadership, especially as it impacts the process of simplification.

Ted Chung of Hyundai Card is convinced that the reinvention of his
company could not have happened without his top-down management
style. Further, he believes that leader-driven companies tend to be more
successful, even when they're not operating in crisis mode. Ted says:

*If you want to be just a good company, you can be leader-driven or col-
laborative. But to be a great company, you need a good leader and a
top-down-driven organization.*

Three hours from Copenhagen, in Bjerringbro, Denmark, is the headquarters of a fascinating company called Grundfos. Its business is devoted
to the availability of one of the world's most precious resources: water.
Grundfos designs and sells water pumps. It is no small business, with a
global workforce of eighteen thousand employees and annual sales over
twelve million units.

CEO Niels Due Jensen has a deep-seated belief that top-down management is what keeps a company simple. He thinks it's the leader's challenge to find new ways to simplify and the most efficient way to keep things
simple as the company moves forward.

*Input is valuable, but you need a captain on the bridge. You don't need
ten captains to point the direction a company should be sailing. Steve Jobs
had people to tell him what course to take, but he was the one who made
the decisions.*

Niels's idea of a leader who values simplicity is the no-nonsense type—
one who is driven by vision, taste, boldness, and common sense.

As the son of Grundfos's founder, Niels makes a distinction between a leader who founds or owns a company and one who is hired for the job. When you are both owner and leader, it's easier to take risks. You accept responsibility and take the blame if the risk doesn't pay off. Leaders who are hired from the outside are typically less willing to make the bolder or riskier decision. They're more protective, which introduces an element of complexity. The clear, bold path becomes fuzzier and more open to debate.

Does that mean an outsider is doomed to failure in the effort to simplify? Not at all. It just means that it's difficult to lead for simplicity when you're looking over your shoulder. A degree of boldness is necessary for the job.

In Niels's view the challenge in large companies is to build a culture that creates leaders who, through a combination of bravery and common sense, can make those tough decisions. Leaders must be made to feel that they have the company's support, or they will hesitate to make the risky decision—even if it might be the company's best chance to reach greater heights.

In 2011 the drama of an outsider being asked to reinvent a company played out on a rather large stage, with a not-so-happy ending. For every fan of simplicity it serves as a cautionary tale.

When Leading for Simplicity Failed: The JCPenney Story

Unfortunately, the love of simplicity alone is not enough to slay the beast of complexity. The adventures of Ron Johnson are proof of that.

Earlier we heard how Ron leveraged the power of simplicity to take the retail Apple Stores from concept to reality. Steve Jobs had recruited Ron because he wanted someone with a brilliant retail brain and a passion for excellence, and Ron's experience as vice president of merchandising with the U.S. retail chain Target made him the perfect candidate for the role. Under Ron's leadership Target morphed from an average department store to a far more popular and tasteful one. (Given its shift to higher quality, many jokingly Frenchified the store's name, pronouncing it "Tar-ZHAY.")

As leader of Apple's retail effort, Ron achieved even greater success and quite a bit of fame in the process. During his tenure, he helped create a network of more than three hundred Apple Stores in prime locations around the world, featuring stunning architecture, beautifully designed interiors, and an abundance of helpful employees.

His experience made Ron very attractive to JCPenney, a huge and once-great chain of American department stores, which recruited Ron to become its new CEO in 2011. Ron's love of simplicity served him very well at Apple and Target, yet at JCPenney it never seemed to gain traction at all. The company lost nearly $1 *billion* in a single year, and Ron parted ways with JCPenney after only eighteen months on the job.

In this particular tale I will serve not only as your humble narrator but also as an eyewitness—or, depending on your point of view, an accomplice. I was one of the people Ron recruited to help with JCPenney's rebranding and advertising when he accepted the job. I was part of a small group called The Bureau, made up of seven individuals who had worked together in previous adventures creating branding and advertising for Apple and other iconic brands.

The JCPenney board brought Ron in as CEO because the brand was in need of serious reinvention. In fact, the very concept of the American department store was in need of reinvention. Many of the big names in retail were being hurt by the Internet and by customers' growing interest in specialty shops. JCPenney, unfortunately, had it particularly bad. Unlike department stores like Macy's and H&M, it suffered from the image of being "Grandma's store." It had become stale over a long period of time. Trying to keep up with the other guys, JCPenney was using the same weapons they were using—a barrage of sales and coupons—and the battle wasn't going well.

JCPenney still had a core group of devoted shoppers, but those people were actually part of the problem. Sales and coupons be damned, the JCPenney fans just weren't spending enough. Sales figures were trending in the wrong direction. If the store was to succeed in the long term, it needed to attract younger and more affluent customers.

With his stellar résumé, JCPenney thought Ron would be its savior.

Wall Street strongly agreed. The company's stock rose 17 percent on the news of Ron's appointment.

Then it was time to get to work. When Ron arrived at JCPenney, he found stores that were cluttered with merchandise—much of it not the most stylish or the highest quality—and no real pricing policy other than sale, sale, sale. There was no future vision at work, and previous efforts to revitalize the JCPenney brand had only sputtered.

All eyes were on Ron to come up with an inspiring vision that would not only pump up sales but also chart the course for a new, more vibrant, more appealing JCPenney.

What Ron had in mind was simplification on a massive scale. Rather than make people jump through hoops to get the best prices, he'd do away with sales and coupons and give them low prices every day. Rather than make customers work hard to find "the good stuff," he'd phase out the questionable goods and bring in quality products from the most respected and popular names in fashion and design.

Ron's initial plans for JCPenney were, unsurprisingly, based on what he had observed in the success of the Apple Stores. Those stores were always packed, even though everything sold there could be purchased more conveniently online. The reason: Apple Stores offered a shopping experience that could not be duplicated online. People wanted to go to the store to try things out and ask questions of people who really knew the products. Many would go simply because it was an interesting place to hang out and use the Internet.

This same philosophy would guide a new approach to selling at JCPenney. It would be all about the customer experience. Ron's plan was to again create an experience that could not be found on the Internet or in competitors' stores.

He found inspiration in the philosophy of the company's founder, James Cash Penney, who based his selling philosophy on respect for the customer. Penney didn't believe in gimmicks and sales. He named his first stores The Golden Rule, because he was passionate about treating customers as he wished to be treated himself.

Ron aimed to bring that philosophy front and center again. Not only would he offer high-quality products from around the world at attractive prices, but he would also put an end to the traditional department-store trickery of door-buster sales and mailboxes full of coupons. Surely people understood that those discounts weren't "real." The stores play games with initial pricing in order to be able to blare, "40% OFF!" a week later. In contrast, everything about the new JCPenney would be built around respect for the customer.

At a big-production event on a rented pier in New York City, Ron unveiled his vision to an invitation-only crowd of industry analysts and journalists. The next day Wall Street responded enthusiastically, driving JCPenney's stock price up another 24 percent.

The experts were convinced. Ron was poised to deliver. Simplicity was about to win again. The JCPenney brand had punched its ticket to a whole new future.

Or not.

Fast-forward eighteen months: Ron and JCPenney severed their relationship amid scathing reviews and horrific losses. How the heck did that happen? Ron's story is a valuable one for anyone who sets out to simplify.

First, know that Ron is an easy man to work with. His personality is light-years away from that of his former boss Steve Jobs. He loves rolling up his sleeves with a group and coming up with creative solutions. He thrives when he has honest interactions with his staff, as he did at Apple.

However, at Apple Ron built his staff from scratch. At JCPenney he was walking into a hundred-year-old company with a large, multilayered staff that was firmly entrenched. Rather than nuke the joint, Ron explains, he chose to build a "quilt" of old and new. He wanted to bring in some new blood with a fresh perspective but felt an obligation to keep people who had tied their careers and families to the success of the company for so many years.

Injected into this existing organization, Ron had trouble establishing an honest communication loop with some of the existing staff. He recalls a conversation with Safra Catz, copresident and CFO of Oracle, on this very topic. Oracle had bought a number of companies, including People-Soft, and Safra was well experienced in the art of merging existing cultures with new leadership. She cautioned Ron that if there were leaders in the old organization who didn't agree with his ways, they could well take down the entire transformation with their passive-aggressive behavior.

Trying to build that quilt of old and new did indeed have some unpleasant side effects. It created a problem with internal communications and getting everyone on the same page.

Meanwhile, development of the new JCPenney was moving forward. On the top floor of a JCPenney store in a dying Dallas mall, Ron built a secret prototype store for a whole new JCPenney. With the help of terrifically talented designers and architects, he finessed his vision for a reimagined department store experience. What Ron and his team created was decidedly not "Grandma's store."

It was a stunning sight. Spacious aisles connected a village of boutique shops, each featuring a popular brand, staffed by experts who could knowledgeably answer customers' questions. There was a coffee shop, a candy store, and computer tables where shoppers could take care of personal matters or even compare JCPenney's prices with those of its competitors. There were counters throughout the store where customers could get expert advice on decorating, party preparations, and many other home endeavors.

Most of the people who walked away from the prototype store felt they had just seen the rebirth of the department store. There was value for existing customers plus an amazing new shopping experience for the younger and more affluent customers JCPenney needed to attract.

The plan was taking shape. You could see the future unfolding. Unfortunately, there was a large problem brewing simultaneously, and it was of Ron's own making. He now refers to it as his "fatal flaw."

The massive physical changes to the stores would take years to complete—yet Ron plunged right in by cutting the sales and coupons. He was eager to implement the "everyday low price" strategy that was a cornerstone of his reinvention vision, even though it would be some time before the physical appearance of the stores and the merchandise for sale delivered on the vision.

Feeling betrayed by the sudden loss of sales and coupons, the traditional shoppers stayed away in droves. Without a compelling visible reason to check out the stores, the new generation of younger shoppers didn't show up. It was a double whammy for the company, and one from which it couldn't recover.

Ron has since done a lot of reflecting about the failure of JCPenney's reinvention and where he went wrong.

I think we had a really terrific vision. Most people agree with that. But there was one fatal flaw in execution, and that was timing. We went too fast for employees, customers, board members, and shareholders.

The banishing of sales and coupons started the wagon rolling downhill, out of control. Though the new pricing policy was more respectful of the shoppers' time and money, those same shoppers had been conditioned over the decades to respond to sales and coupons—even if they perceived them as a bit of a shell game.

We might have said, "Let's go to everyday low pricing, but let's also keep the coupons going for a while to transition customers to a better way of finding value." But we didn't. We moved way too fast, and that set us up to fail.

Once the damage caused by the new pricing plan became apparent, many critics blamed it on the obvious: a lack of research. If Ron wanted to know how customers would respond to the changes, all he had to do was ask. Why didn't he? Was it because he was an Apple guy, and Apple didn't believe in consumer research? The failure to test appears to be a grave oversight.

That may be true, but hindsight is a wonderful thing. Remember, the eleven members of the JCPenney board, all experts in the industry, thought the plan was genius. So did Wall Street. So did the industry observers who attended Ron's grand unveiling. Just about everyone in and around JCPenney accepted as fact that customers love honesty. But the buck stops in the CEO's office, which turned out to be a place Ron occupied only briefly.

I put the question to Ron directly: Why the lack of basic customer research?

I relied on the idea that half of America shops at JCPenney and that people value the truth. I believed that when we told our customers the truth about our new pricing, why it's more honest, and why it's to their benefit, they'd respond well. That would have enabled us to add all these new customers who didn't like that old coupon thing.

The extreme drop in sales took its toll. The board, which originally supported a transformation plan that would take several years, didn't exactly display steely resolve when sales tanked. On one hand, a change of heart when the losses became greater than expected is understandable. On the other, the board abandoned ship on a plan it had enthusiastically approved. When the going got tough, Ron's relationship with the board became strained. He recalls:

I told the board, "Although the year was tougher than anticipated, and the skeptics are getting louder, we will succeed. However, you seem uncomfortable with this transformation, so you need to make a critical choice. You can stay on the highway, and we'll slow down to make the necessary changes. Or you can do a U-turn and try to find the customer we've left behind."

The board decided to take the U-turn. In fact, it did more than a U-turn. It got off the highway and started to search for a customer who no longer exists.

At the time this book was written, more than two years after Ron and JCPenney parted ways, the board's search had still not borne fruit. The door-buster sales, coupons, and endless email pitches came back stronger than ever—but the shoppers did not. And, even if JCPenney succeeds in turning back the clock to the time before Ron, it will find itself in the same predicament that caused it to hire Ron in the first place. It will be in need of innovative thinking to attract a younger, more affluent audience.

Today's JCPenney seems to be looking for a formula that will magically attract more shoppers. But seemingly endless changes—management, logos, ads, and theme lines—only serve to confuse customers. The lack of focus and direction weakens the brand rather than strengthens it. This is simplicity's old foe, complexity, doing what it does best.

Leading for Simplicity, Aiming for Outcomes

Speaking at the British Embassy's Creative Summit in 2012, Apple's chief designer, Jony Ive, made a point about Apple's priorities.

"We are really pleased with our revenues," he said, "but our goal isn't to make money. It sounds a little flippant, but it's the truth. Our goal, and what makes us excited, is to make great products. If we are successful, people will like them—and if we are operationally competent, we will make money."

Apple's detractors may scoff at the idea that Apple's goal isn't to make money. After all, in mid-2015, Apple's cash reserves topped $200 billion. But seeing profit as a consequence of making great products is a very different philosophy from prioritizing profit. It has a tremendous effect on the decisions leaders make and the overall way they run a business.

Based on my own experience in technology marketing, I believe Jony accurately states the difference between Apple and others in the industry. In meetings with executives at Dell and Intel in the process of developing advertising, conversations about generating website clicks and boosting profits were far more common than talk about doing world-changing work. In contrast, I never attended a single meeting at Apple that focused on jacking up profits. Our focus was doing our part to help create Steve's intended outcome, which was winning the hearts of customers. In our dealings with Steve, there was never any question that profit was the consequence of excellent work, not the cause.

Australian job-placement entrepreneur Andrew Bassat, CEO of SEEK, echoes Jony's comment about choosing the right goals.

> *What we communicate is pretty simple. What we try to achieve as an organization is not about making money. It's much more about creating desired outcomes. We've mostly gotten it right. The few times we started focusing on making money, we've actually gone a bit astray. If one creates a great business—in our case, a marketplace for job seekers and companies looking for staff—the profit will follow. So that's what we focus on.*

StubHub cofounder Jeff Fluhr's take is that you can't build a successful company if your priority is short-term revenue. He takes the long view—thinking about what consumers want, designing a product, and continuing to iterate, tweak, and evolve until the product delivers real value. That's the natural order of things: create a product of value, and then value creates profit.

StubHub had the good fortune to generate revenue from the start, because the company received a percentage of every ticket sold. However, many of today's more successful companies—including Facebook, Twitter, Pinterest, Snapchat, and WhatsApp—did not have that kind of direct income early on. Their business model was to create the outcome, and that outcome led to revenue.

The leaders I spoke to overwhelmingly endorse the notion of aiming for outcomes, for big and small companies alike. Challenged to create an outcome, a workforce is both unified and inspired.

Leading for outcomes is not only more heroic—it's also more effective.

Chapter 4
Simplicity Is a Team Sport

No question, a strong leader is simplicity's greatest asset.

That said, leadership does not occur in a vacuum. Business leaders are only as effective as the management team they recruit and the workforce they shape.

Every organization has its own methods for finding the people who will best advance the company's mission. Some look for specific skills and experience, while others put chemistry and cultural fit high on their priority list.

I was curious to learn how business leaders who believe in the power of simplicity go about the business of hiring. Do they look for a particular kind of person? How do they find, train, and empower them? How quick are they to replace employees who perform poorly?

Like many, Steve Jobs believed that a company is only as good as its people. His no-compromise approach to products and principles carried over to his hiring practices. When you worked for Steve, you had to be in sync with Steve's values—his work ethic, his vision, and his love of innovation, design, and simplicity. He wasn't looking for people to agree with him, but he did want people who were aligned with his core beliefs. That's an important distinction.

Although Steve was a tough boss, he was also a superb one. The reason he hired brilliant and creative people was that he wanted them to be brilliant and creative. He was there to provide the unifying vision and to coordinate the efforts of many disciplines.

As has been frequently reported, Steve's guidance could be delivered in forceful ways, which often resulted in spirited debate. That was Steve's way of ensuring that the Apple workplace was one in which the best ideas rose to the top. It took a certain kind of person to thrive in that atmosphere.

Business leaders who believe in simplicity have different ideas about how they find and hire those who share their values and how they free themselves from those who aren't performing to the company's standards. Some have a formalized system for hiring. Others don't, relying on intuition over formal processes to staff their teams.

John McGrath, for example, says he makes most of his hiring decisions based on a gut feeling. When candidates come in for interviews, he doesn't read CVs. He assumes that his HR people have already satisfied themselves at that level of detail. John just wants to meet a person for five minutes to see if he gets excited in their company.

StubHub cofounder Jeff Fluhr started with a formalized process but his personal hiring criteria changed over the years. In the company's earliest days, his recruitment philosophy was based on what he'd observed in the business world in general. It was very logical. For example, if he was looking for a business-to-business marketing person, he would tell his recruiters that he was looking for someone who knew online and offline marketing, was good at brand messaging, and could build a strong team. The recruiters would search for those whose experience checked all the boxes. Jeff would then meet with the top three candidates and, he hoped, find one he liked.

Now Jeff thinks he had it backward with that approach.

In certain situations it's important to find someone who fills a certain skill set. But more often it's about finding someone who's got more of the nature

85

and innate qualities you're looking for—things like intelligence, curiosity, creativity, cultural fit, and work ethic.

If you find someone who possesses these traits, says Jeff, even if they've done only a few of the things you want them to do, they'll likely be an excellent hire because they're smart, hardworking, and motivated. People like that can figure things out pretty quickly and they fit well with the team.

He points out that there are definitely times when you would *not* want to recruit this way. If you need a heart surgeon, for example, being nice, creative, and curious isn't likely to offset a lack of experience. Still, there's value in recruiting for fit with the culture and company, not just for experience.

I just think that in a lot of these roles—nontechnical roles and even some technical ones—it should be more about personal traits than "Have they done the seventeen things that I need this person to do?"

Jeff's priorities in hiring were echoed by many of the leaders I interviewed, in the sense that intelligence and shared values were more important than checking off items on a résumé. A company that believes in the power of simplicity needs to satisfy itself that new hires will thrive in the culture of simplicity and positively influence those who join the company later.

At SEEK in Australia, CEO Andrew Bassat talked about the moment he realized how important it was to hire for shared values. Facing rapid growth, his organization was staffing quickly and in the process brought on some less-than-ideal people. Andrew found that the culture was being adversely affected by these people. Some were creating friction in the workplace and others just didn't share the goals of their coworkers. He realized that finding people whose values matched those of the company was every bit as important as finding people who performed well. He lost his tolerance for those who were out of sync with the company's values, no matter how good they were at their jobs.

Still, even among those who passionately believe in the value of simplicity there are different ways of finding the "right" people.

Brilliant Hires Are the Key

No one will ever know exactly what went through Steve Jobs's mind when it came to hiring the best and brightest—other than the fact that he sometimes mentioned that hiring brilliant people was his most important job.

But many, including Ron Johnson, know what it was like to go through the process of being interviewed and hired by Steve. Ron and Steve had a brief courtship period before Ron finally joined the company to head the development of the Apple Stores.

Perhaps unsurprisingly, Steve's approach in hiring Ron was similar to the method by which he lured John Sculley away from Pepsi many years earlier. You're probably familiar with Steve's famous line to Sculley: "Do you want to sell sugar water or do you want to change the world?" (A fantastic line, even if Steve would later regret sealing the deal with Sculley.)

Preferring to hire people who were already rock stars in their fields, Steve was drawn to Ron because of his impressive résumé.

Ron met Steve only twice before he was offered the job, spending about four hours with him in total, which is consistent with many people's accounts about how quickly Steve formed opinions. On the first night Ron and Steve talked for two hours, getting to know each other better. That went well enough to merit a second meeting.

In that second meeting Steve became the salesman. He acknowledged to Ron that he'd done a terrific job building the Target brand, and then he quietly began the pitch. "But you know Apple," he said. "We change the world."

Steve built upon that theme, talking about how Apple was pushing the world forward with such products as iMovie, which allowed ordinary people to turn raw video into high-quality movies with special effects and professional titling. He talked about how Apple products were influencing the way people lived, worked, invented, and played all over the world.

To Steve, Apple's mission not only propelled the company forward but also served as a persuasive recruiting tool. Steve did his best to make Ron feel that with Apple he would be signing on for an important, life-changing adventure.

That was how Steve zeroed in on someone he had already identified as a potentially prime asset to the company. But how did he go about filling a job when he had no specific person in mind? I had a personal experience with Steve that answered that question, and I have to give him points for originality. I'd never seen this done before.

One day, after my time as creative director at Apple's ad agency, I received a phone call from Steve. He told me that he wanted to replace his VP of marketing and was looking for candidates. The interesting part was that he didn't want a bunch of names. He wanted only one. He wanted to know who was the smartest marketing person I'd ever worked with, period. He was obviously making the same call to a number of people, and this was his way of starting his search with the cream of the crop and distilling from there.

The one name I gave was Stephen Sonnenfeld, someone I had worked with on the IBM, Intel, and Dell advertising accounts. I told Steve that Sonnenfeld knew the industry inside and out and, equally important, was a champion of outstanding creative work. Because he earned the respect of his clients, he had the ability to push back against their objections without alienating them.

Jobs called Sonnenfeld. I'd failed to tell Sonnenfeld he'd be calling, so it came as a bit of a shock. In fact, like many who have received the "Hi, this is Steve Jobs" call, Sonnenfeld was sure it was a joke. However, after a brief conversation Jobs invited Sonnenfeld to Cupertino to meet in person. Sonnenfeld agreed, even though he had only recently taken a job leading the advertising effort for JPMorgan Chase.

A few days later he received a plane ticket along with an agenda that had him meeting with Jobs, an HR person, Phil Schiller (head of product marketing), Ron Johnson (then head of Apple retail), and Apple's ad agency leaders, Lee Clow and James Vincent.

Now, if you were interviewing for a job with most big companies, you'd probably meet with a number of people before you were cleared to meet with the CEO. That's not the way it worked in this instance. Jobs wanted to meet Sonnenfeld first.

Sonnenfeld describes arriving at Apple's campus, being led to the conference room next to Jobs's office, and being told that Jobs would be right in.

Steve strode into the room in full costume—black turtleneck, jeans, New Balances—then gave me a cordial "hello" and got right down to business.

Jobs inquired about Sonnenfeld's current job, running the JPMorgan Chase advertising account for a hot upstart agency. Sonnenfeld was proud of the work, but Jobs made it clear that he didn't hold banks, as institutions, in very high regard. When Sonnenfeld explained how the bank was helping communities, Jobs said, "Anyone can throw money at things. What are they doing that's really good for the world?"

That opening volley put Sonnenfeld in defense mode. Then, as he recalls, Jobs zeroed in on the ten years he'd spent working the IBM and Intel accounts.

For Steve, seeing these experiences on my résumé was like a shark circling his bloody prey. He said, "You haven't really been associated with any great work during your career."

Now squarely on the ropes, Sonnenfeld attempted to defend what he'd done on both pieces of business. Jobs would have none of it. What Sonnenfeld cited as decent work Jobs derided as crap. He kept asking why Sonnenfeld wasn't able to make the marketing better.

Exasperated, Sonnenfeld tried to pull out of this death spiral, explaining that he'd done the best work under the circumstances but that JPMorgan Chase was a big, complicated company. Therefore, the work didn't fully represent who he was or what he was capable of.

> *Jobs sat silent for several beats and then came back with the statement that will be forever cemented in my head. He said, "Yeah, I have a problem with the work, but that's not what really concerns me. What I can't accept is that you were able to do this for so many years and still get up in the morning and look at yourself in the mirror."*
>
> *I was stunned. It was the interview equivalent of a knockout. My meeting with Steve quickly came to a close.*

Even though that meeting did not go well, Sonnenfeld still went on to meet the others as scheduled. Perhaps Steve still wanted to get others' opinions. Back in New York two days later, Sonnenfeld sent Jobs the obligatory thank-you email.

> *Within minutes Steve shot back, "Thanks for coming out. I don't think that you're right for the position." But that had already been made abundantly clear.*
>
> *I was trying to justify my role in a group process by explaining that the dynamics forced compromise. Steve not only couldn't understand that, it seemed that he couldn't even acknowledge the concept of compromise or respect anyone who was forced to accept compromise when it degraded the work. It hit me that there were very few people in the world like this, let alone heads of major companies.*

Just a few months after Sonnenfeld's day of disappointment in Cupertino, Jobs delivered his famous commencement address at Stanford University. In that speech he said, "You've got to find what you love. The only way to be truly satisfied is to do what you believe is great work. And the only way to do great work is to love what you do."

Today, as vice president of advertising and brand integration at Thomson Reuters, Sonnenfeld is still moved by that speech, his feelings amplified by his personal adventure with Jobs. Though he might not have fit at Apple, he feels transformed by his brush with Steve Jobs and the man's unwavering principles.

Jobs had a crystal clear vision for the type of company Apple would be, and he was very particular about finding employees who fit into that vision. He looked for brilliant and talented people who were as uncompromising about quality as he was, but, just as important, he was also looking for people who were willing to take responsibility. At the management level Apple was free of the complex processes and hierarchies so common in other global companies, because Steve hired people he could trust to perform.

The leaders who participated in this book have a number of different approaches to hiring, but all agreed that recruitment is a critical part of keeping things simple. Employing people who share your values is the best way to move a company forward—and keep complexity at bay.

"People Are the Whole Ball Game"

Ron Johnson has a personal set of standards when it comes to hiring and the way he likes to work with people. He attributes his past successes to the relationships he built with his teams.

Ron claims to have only one overall requirement for his direct reports: "Tell me what you think." That may sound simple, but if you've spent years working in big companies, you know that getting honesty out of people isn't always easy. There are often forces at work that prevent them from being straightforward, says Ron, including fear of losing their jobs, desire to gain favor, avoidance of conflict, and so on.

> *There are two ways you can go with business associates—you can have a relationship or you can have an arrangement. In a relationship people tell*

each other what they think. It may not be comfortable all the time, but you learn from each other and you grow from it. An arrangement is something where people place greater value on their personal safety and security. They don't tell the truth. They tell you what you want to hear.

Ron says that this was one key difference between his time at Apple and his time at JCPenney. Building the Apple retail group from the ground up involved a lot of people working together to create something new. Ron was accessible and encouraged honesty. He brought the same working values to the position of CEO of JCPenney, but in that company he was the outsider who wanted to change the culture. As a result, he couldn't get beyond "arrangements" with some people, and that contributed to the complexity of his job.

CEO Kip Tindell of The Container Store also talks quite a bit about the importance of relationships—both those between himself and his direct reports and peer-to-peer relationships between members of his executive team. He believes it's the quality of the employees that differentiates his company from its competitors, so he attributes much of The Container Store's success to its ability to find, hire, and retain a certain type of person.

Kip looks for people who have a passion for customer service. He goes about finding these people in a way that's open and honest from the start, in the belief that this avoids complications later. He places the highest value on the two traits that most influence business behavior in positive ways.

I believe everything in the world is a kind of commodity, except for judgment and integrity. Lots of people are really smart or athletic or artistic or musical. But judgment and integrity—those things are more rare.

Back in the early days of the company, Kip was personally involved in the hiring of every employee. That's no longer possible, given the size of his organization. Instead, the company has adopted a system by which candidates can be effectively evaluated on those key measures of judgment and integrity.

We interview people to death. We don't do this to be simplistic—we do it because we care so much about hiring the right people. We'll often do seven or eight interviews. And yes, some people think we're weird as heck and take off in the middle of all that.

These interviews come only after people have applied online and answered open-ended questions that give them the opportunity to demonstrate their passion for the brand. Some of the interviews are one-on-one, while others are conducted in a group. This is where the strong culture of The Container Store plays a role, helping the right people succeed and weeding out those who aren't cut out for the experience.

Once people are hired, it's usually pretty easy to tell if they'll fit into the culture. Those who don't will usually leave on their own. They think we're nuts and run off pretty quickly.

Any company can hire a team. What sets the better companies apart is their ability to create a type of perpetual engagement within the team. We're all familiar with the traditional "first days on the job." Typically, you'd experience an orientation day, attending briefings on such topics as work hours, benefits, vacation, and HR policies. At The Container Store your initial experience is quite different.

Once you're on board, you begin what's known as Foundation Week. No matter what your role, you'll spend a whole week in a store, learning the company's selling philosophy and taking a deep dive into the specifics of the business.

As we heard earlier, the Foundation Principles are frequently talked about inside The Container Store, and they are a big part of this training period. It's important for new hires to appreciate why they're being asked to conduct themselves in certain ways. It's not about becoming some sort of drone, assimilated into the hive—it's about truly understanding the unique shopping experience that distinguishes The Container Store.

One of the Foundation Principles sums up the reason this lengthy training process exists. It's the idea that when the company hires the right person—someone who is energetic, intelligent, and hardworking—that person will do the work of three.

Training doesn't stop after Foundation Week. While the average retailer conducts eight hours of formal training within the span of a year for new employees, The Container Store provides an average of 263 hours. Kip says that this is done to develop the skills of those who are hired and to retain them.

We make this investment in first-year training because there's nothing worse than being put onto a retail sales floor without knowing anything about the products. That's just cruel.

If you think The Container Store is beginning to sound like a cult, you're not entirely mistaken. What you're really seeing is a super strong culture at work. This kind of deeply embedded culture is something you find at Apple, Google, Nike, and any other successful company where people are encouraged to thrive as individuals and also work together to meet the company's goals. It's not for everyone, which is why those who don't fit in tend to leave quickly.

Surprisingly, considering the number of employees required to smoothly run so many large stores in so many places, The Container Store doesn't do its recruiting with a traditional HR department. To find the quantity of high-quality people needed, management instead asks the company's employees to do the recruiting. Wherever they meet smart, passionate people, they're encouraged to drop the hint. It might be someone who waits on them in a restaurant. Or someone they meet on a rock music cruise. Or even that remote relative they just bumped into at a holiday dinner, says Kip.

We don't have any rules against having family work for us. Bring us your great-aunts, uncles, and cousins. That's how we populate the company.

The Container Store puts a huge amount of energy into making employees feel like part of the company. Kip believes that when employees have a sense of belonging, they tend to talk about their work to friends and family. Sometimes that plants a seed in people's minds that maybe they'd like to work in a place like that too.

Though the cost of bringing people into the company is high, it's a cost Kip is happy to pay. The Container Store has one of the highest SGAs (sales, general, and administrative expenses) in the entire retail industry. But the store also has one of the highest gross margins in the industry, which mitigates that expense.

> *We're just passionate. When you look at the amount of training we do over the years, it goes up and up and up. It's also the best money we've ever spent—a blend of science and art.*

That big investment in first-year training for new employees continues to pay dividends. In their second year employees take pride in mentoring the next batch of new hires, so that higher training expense comes with its own form of ROI.

When you add all this together—the recruiting, the training, the culture, the communication—it leads directly to higher employee productivity, which in turn leads to greater customer happiness.

Lou Carbone, an academic in the field of customer and employee experience, once wrote that the first 25 percent of any employee's effort is devoted to basic productivity. This is the minimum effort required to do their job. If they don't perform at this level, they'll be fired. The remaining 75 percent of their effort is purely voluntary. How much of this extra effort employees give depends on how much they like what they're selling, how they feel about their boss, their working conditions, the corporate mission, and so on.

Kip estimates that most retailers get only slightly more than the basic 25 percent effort from employees but that The Container Store enjoys employee productivity in the 80 percent range. He's convinced that his company's method of finding, training, and keeping people really works—and keeping the workforce engaged and fulfilled is what makes a company successful.

How Much Does Loyalty Cost?

Some people work because they love their jobs. For them, the money is actually secondary. Steve Jobs was famous for taking a one-dollar annual salary upon his return to Apple in 1997, reportedly just so he could be an official employee and enjoy the benefits of health insurance coverage. I've often wondered if he got a rate-of-inflation raise the following year.

That kind of commitment is admirable, but for the rest of us substantial compensation is a nice thing to have. Not only do we like a good salary, but we also tend to jump through hoops when an additional reward is dangled before us. The question is, when you give employees that special reward—a bonus—could you be rewarding the wrong thing?

At SEEK in Australia, CEO Andrew Bassat says he's eliminated short-term bonuses entirely. In fact, it's been quite liberating, he says. This action was based on his observation that people promised a bonus for delivering some short-term result tended to think in the short term. Andrew saw this as somewhat superficial and not the kind of thinking that would propel SEEK into the future.

Clearly this is an area worthy of debate. Companies give people bonuses for different reasons and therefore derive different results. But there are some lessons in simplicity to be learned from the variety of ways people get compensated.

Dell is my favorite example of a company that has institutionalized a certain kind of disunity. It is composed of a number of separate, distinct divisions, each with its own P&L. The executives in those divisions receive bonuses based on the performance of their own division. Thus there is every incentive to make sales soar in their own division and little incentive to work on behalf of the overall Dell brand. This type of setup promotes disparate perceptions of the company by different divisions, which creates a certain friction that impedes the progress of the overall Dell brand.

As evidence, consider that until 2010 the business and consumer divisions of Dell each used different logos on their computers, as well as in their advertising. No one seemed to care that there were tens of millions of people using Dell computers at home and in the office, and that they were seeing two companies when they should have been seeing one. How this was allowed to go on for so many years is inexplicable.

Over at Apple there are no separate P&Ls. There is Apple. Every executive has an area of responsibility that contributes to the companywide bottom line. Rewards normally come in the form of stock options, which means that individuals in different groups all benefit when the overall performance of the company is good. When the goal is building one powerful brand, a unified company is a simpler way to get there.

You may remember that Steve Jobs found himself in hot water for Apple's practice of backdating stock options given to key employees as incentives. It was an illegal corporate behavior, and part of the fallout was the departure of two members of Apple's executive team. However, the principles behind this practice are hard to argue—and perfectly legal when implemented correctly. Steve understood how important it was to incentivize key employees to remain with the company. When a new batch of stock options is maturing every year, it becomes difficult to walk away.

Back in the late eighties I had the pleasure of being on the receiving end of one of Steve's offers and had Steve's compensation philosophy delivered to me personally. I was his ad agency creative director at the time, working on the NeXT Computer business. After a couple of years, when we had developed a good working relationship, Steve invited me into his office for a private chat.

I sat in the chair in front of his desk and was surprised when he offered me the job of internal creative director at NeXT. We talked about the nature of the job for about thirty minutes and, since things seemed to be going well, the topic then turned to money. Steve looked straight at me and said, "What do you make now, about two hundred thousand dollars?"

I was making nothing of the sort. But since Steve seemed to believe it, I did my best to act as if I were. I responded with a casual "Yes, that's about right." For that brief instant I fantasized that Steve was about to offer even more than my imaginary salary.

Instead he said, "Well, I can't give you that." The dream deflated. But, without skipping a beat, he went on to explain that what he was offering was better than a big check. My memory is that it went like this: "You will never build true wealth by salary alone. No matter how big your monthly checks are, that money will disappear. House, life expenses, vacations, all that stuff. What you really want is equity in the company, and that's what I can give you. That way, you'll make a good salary for a great company doing amazing things, and you'll be building wealth through equity as you do that."

Convincing as that might have been, I had to decline for personal reasons. However, I still have flashes of an alternate reality in which I accepted Steve's offer and am now retired in my castle in England.

The important point is that motivation matters. It's easy to fill offices with people who want a job. The challenge is finding people who believe in the company's mission. They're the ones who will be motivated to help build the company's future—not just pay their bills today.

Who Do You Want in the Boat?

Ron Johnson has his own observations about Steve Jobs's hiring philosophy and the way he'd interact with his managers.

As we saw in Stephen Sonnenfeld's story, Steve could be pretty brutal when he interviewed job candidates. It was his way of testing people to find the special few—those who were brilliant in their area of expertise, eager to work hard, passionate enough to make personal sacrifices, and willing to fight for what they believed in.

Steve didn't feel that a company needed an army of people to be successful. Remember, he had an aversion to large bureaucratic organizations. Ron recalls:

Steve would start every new project by asking, "Who do I want in the boat with me on this one? If I'm in a crisis and I need help rowing the boat, who would I pick?" So he was very good at figuring out "who's in." And the fewer people he could get by with, the better it would be.

Steve had an aversion to working with middlemen, Ron says. He wanted to have direct relationships with the talented people who did the creating and not have to go through their handlers. That's what I observed throughout my own involvement with Steve as well. Anyone who wasn't an active participant in a project was not welcome in our regular meetings. Ron continues:

When we were designing a glass stairway at one of our Apple Stores, Steve wanted to talk to the person who did the design. He wanted to get to the structural engineer and debate. He never wanted to talk to intermediaries.

Steve respected doers. He respected creators. Those are the people he spent his time with, and he didn't much tolerate others. And he had a great nose for those who were lightweight and somewhat political. He could see right through them.

Steve valued intelligence, says Ron, but he also judged people on their ability to communicate. If you couldn't communicate clearly, he didn't think you were very smart. He had no patience for people who weren't clear in expressing their thoughts.

Another part of Steve's brilliance was his exceptional ability to delegate. That would allow him to stay focused on the things he could add value to.

Steve ran a functional organization, relying on those he selected to run their own organizations within Apple. That's why he had Tim Cook taking care of operations, Fred Anderson running the finances, and Ron Johnson taking care of retail. Steve would float in when a new product was being developed, or if he sensed there was a problem that needed his attention. Ron explains:

In any other situation he let people do their thing. He didn't waste any time on it. He had no involvement. Zero. But he had such high standards, and he made his standards so clear to the people he empowered, they could think like him even if he wasn't there.

He said, "I'm going to spend a lot of time with you, because I want to teach you how I think. Once you understand that and you know my standards, you'll be free as a bird. You'll only come to me if there's an issue, or when you want to ask my opinion about something."

Steve would call Ron about five nights a week. In general, Steve would ask, "How was your day? What are you thinking? What did you learn today?" It was his way of deepening their working relationship as they conceived and built the Apple Stores. Through these conversations Ron came to understand Steve's thinking, what he valued, and what he did not.

After selecting a few retail locations together, Ron appreciated Steve's thinking about real estate. After they designed a few stores together, he got a better idea of the materials Steve liked and his feelings about design. Once he had gained this knowledge, it was just as Steve said it would be—he trusted Ron to oversee operations in a way that was aligned with his values. In many ways, Ron says, working with Steve was a liberating experience.

That last comment is important, because it runs contrary to the perception that Steve was a micromanager. People might have had some fear about how Steve would respond to something, but they also knew that what he really wanted to see was something fresh and wonderful. Steve could be disappointed if you *didn't* spread your wings.

As time went on, Ron would have only a few meetings each year with Steve relating to the newest Apple Stores. He'd show Steve the stores in progress and Steve would offer up his reactions and suggestions.

He wasn't heavily involved in the normal sense of that word—but when he walked through a store, you'd never seen such attention to detail.

This working philosophy was key to Steve's success during his second act at Apple. Understanding his own limits, he surrounded himself with people who had strengths he did not. He created an environment in which his hires could be bold and creative. But his vision was ever present, whether it showed up as high-level guidance or a perfectionist's eye for detail.

Clearly, finding the right people is critical for every company. However, a company's workforce is defined not only by those who are hired but also by those who are asked to leave.

The Art of Firing

TBWA\Chiat\Day has been involved with Apple's advertising since the days of the Apple II computer in the late 1970s, when it was called Chiat\Day.

Founder Jay Chiat, who passed away in 2002, was a larger-than-life figure who had a huge influence on the world of advertising. Jay was a creative leader who could focus people in a way that helped them accomplish amazing things. The roster of accounts won and served well by Chiat\Day for more than twenty-five years was beyond impressive, including such companies as Nike, Porsche, Nissan, Energizer, Reebok, American Express, and many more. With great marketing wisdom and a talent for disrupting the industry, Jay was outspoken and highly quotable—so much so that one year the employees of Chiat\Day published a small book for internal distribution entitled *Quotations from Chairman Jay.*

Each page contained a single quote that captured the spirit and wit of the man. There were such gems as "Everything you say is right, but I have a problem with it," "We had an unlimited budget and we exceeded it," and "Well, the next time you tell me something, make sure I listen." My personal favorite, since he once actually said it to me, was "I'm not yelling at you, I'm yelling at the situation."

Being so admired by the advertising community, Jay was invited at one point to write a series of articles for *Adweek* magazine, which at the time was the most widely read industry publication. In this series he shared his wisdom about what makes great agencies great.

One article he wrote has stuck in my mind for decades. Jay opined that in order to build a strong company, one must "fire quickly." His point was that ad agencies are all about relationships, not only with the client but also internally, and our everyday interactions actually define the company. Jay believed that one disgruntled employee would infect those around him with his negativity, and negativity is not a good thing to have in a high-pressure, creative industry.

Jay wasn't a fan of the "two weeks' notice" approach. He'd give some-one two weeks' pay, but that person would be asked to leave immediately. A bit cold, perhaps, but he wanted people to focus on doing their best work in a positive environment. He didn't want one person's bad vibes bringing others down.

Kip Tindell shares similar feelings on the topic of quickly finding and cutting out employees who aren't a good fit with the company, though he puts it in more human terms.

We are compassionate human beings. Or we like to think of ourselves that way. A long time ago we were too damn naively nice about such things, and we used to work, work, work to make a person change [before letting him or her go]. Some traits, particularly the insecurity thing, just can't be changed. Now we're a lot quicker than we used to be.

As we've already seen, a strong culture has the ability to self-regulate. It tends to drive away people who don't belong. But when a leader or store manager is causing a problem within the company and isn't leaving volun-tarily, Kip believes the situation should be addressed with urgency.

Even if a relationship doesn't work out, the manner in which it is re-solved sends a message to everyone about how employees are valued. Kip is proud that even when The Container Store parts ways with people, it does a good job of remaining friends. While he agrees with the Jay Chiat philosophy that bad apples need to be relieved of their duties expeditiously, he disagrees when it comes to the nature of the actual dismissal. The Container Store tends to overpay those who are terminated, says Kip, and typically gives a lot of notice.

Why? In a retail operation like The Container Store, everyone's opinion has an impact on the brand. The people who leave—including those who are asked to leave—are still likely to be customers. They'll be talking about the store to friends and commenting about it online.

So in Kip's thinking, it's fire quickly but don't be heartless about it. It's the human way to behave and it's also better for business.

Of course, a far better idea is to hire more wisely in the first place, which greatly reduces the number of such uncomfortable situations. Once again, values play an important role.

Values Are an Employee Magnet

When a company does a good job of communicating its values, it attracts customers who share those values—and prospective employees as well. Common values are the backbone of a strong, unified team.

For example, social conscience is a fundamental part of the Ben & Jerry's culture, and this is projected in its public image. As a result, the pool of prospective employees is slanted toward people who have a social conscience themselves.

Someone who signs on only because they need a job, and doesn't share the company's values, is likely to find their work challenging and complex. They might be asked to consider things they don't feel appropriate for a business to think about. They'll need to reconcile their personal beliefs with the company's.

Jerry Greenfield says that the company learned the importance of hiring for shared values in its early days of rapid growth, when it was forced to hire many employees in a short period of time. As Jerry laments, the younger versions of themselves weren't quite smart enough to hire for shared values.

Those people tried to change the company to be more like what they're *like. From the outside, Ben & Jerry's appeared to be peace and love, which is good, but [because some of the new hires had different values] there was a fair amount of conflict within—it was a fight for the soul of the company.*

Thankfully, the founders' values prevailed and the social mission became ingrained in the company's DNA. When Ben and Jerry came to realize that the requirements of managing the company had grown beyond their personal capabilities, they took action to expand the management team. At that time, the company's well-known values helped them attract people who were a better fit in the culture.

Today Ben & Jerry's attracts people with a social conscience, just as Apple attracts people who want to create a better world through technology, and just as The Container Store attracts people who are devoted to customer service. Strong values prove to be an effective magnet.

At content-creation company RadicalMedia, cofounders Jon Kamen and Frank Scherma view their principal value—integrity—as the beacon that helps them attract the right talent. In their business especially, the brand *is* the people, so it's critical that they attract and hire high-quality people of like mind.

However, Radical faces a bigger challenge in hiring than many companies because it requires so many different types of people. There are a number of directors attached to the company, support staffers who work full time in the office, and producers and others who are constantly in and out of the building attending to production matters.

The company's strong brand attracts people at every level, but Jon considers one of his most important duties to be the keeper of the sacred flame. He does his best to make sure that new hires are in sync with Radical's values, integrity being value number one. That's not to say they get it right every time, but if a mistake is made, they do their best to make "corrections." Echoing Kip Tindell's feeling, they try to do this gently, because in the world of production it's likely that you'll cross paths again one day. It speaks well for the company, says Jon, that when he encounters people who have been previously cast off, they don't seem to hold a grudge. In fact, most seem to appreciate the time they did spend with Radical.

Because Jon and Frank are protective of their culture, a positive cycle has been repeating at RadicalMedia for many years. New people are attracted to the brand. As employees they work to strengthen the brand. And the stronger brand attracts even more good people to the company.

Simplicity Is a Group Effort

Among companies that benefit from the power of simplicity, we've heard from some that are leader-driven and others that are collaborative. There's no magic formula for leadership.

There is, however, an effective formula for hiring: focusing on people who share the company's values. They're the ones who will not only fit into the culture but will strengthen it as well.

It's also important to note a trend taking place in business today that is disrupting traditional methods of hiring. The on-demand service industry—including such companies as Uber, Postmates, and Munchery—has attracted nearly twenty million people as service providers. The lure for these employees is flexible hours and more control over their lives.

The downside, some argue, is that as this model becomes more popular, workforces become more rootless and less committed. It follows that this new generation of employees is less driven by the company's values and more driven by their own.

Ron Johnson believes there is a "best of both worlds" solution, which he's implemented in his new venture, Enjoy, which launched in mid-2015.

Enjoy presents itself as a better way to buy technology. It curates a selection of high-quality devices (phones, tablets, drones, music systems, cameras, etc.). What differentiates the company from other retailers is that when a customer makes a purchase, Enjoy sends out a qualified expert to hand-deliver the item to the person's home, office, coffee shop, or other chosen location. The expert then spends an hour with the customer to set up the device and show them how to use it, all at no additional cost.

For this on-demand service to be successful, Ron needs Enjoy's workforce to be highly skilled and enthusiastic but also deeply committed to the company's mission. So he literally designed this new on-demand company around its employees. People at Enjoy have the flexibility to work when, where, and how they want, just as at other on-demand services. The difference is that they're all salaried, receiving benefits and company stock. Ron's goal is to give people the freedom and adventure that come with the mobile industry, combined with the security and benefits of the traditional economy.

Once again, Ron is in the "enhancing lives" business. As he did in developing the Apple Store concept, he's searching for people who have a passion for service, and in the process Enjoy is enhancing the lives of customers and employees alike. By structuring the company this way, Ron is putting Enjoy's values front and center. These values are proving to be a magnet for the "right" employees—those who will help build the young company's culture.

As we've seen, when employees' personal values align with the company's, they're more fulfilled, better motivated, and more effective in creating happier customers.

Chapter 5
Simplicity Is True to the Brand

The concept of brand is hardly new. Since the dawn of advertising, agencies have built reputations on their ability to create outstanding brands, because the brand is arguably a company's most valuable property.

At its core, the brand is the sum total of our perceptions of a company. These perceptions come from our personal experience with products, services, retail presence, website, packaging, customer support, and more; the feelings we get from marketing; the impressions we get from news coverage, online and offline; and what we hear from people we trust. The strength of a company's brand comes from many different sources—including some the company cannot directly control.

A strong brand attracts. It wins customers and creates loyalty. When people are ready to buy, they look first at the brands they value most. And they're willing to pay more for a brand they love, because they believe it's worth more.

The mission provides a foundation for the company, and its values guide its actions in fulfilling the mission. But the brand hovers above all these things.

A parallel can be found in our own professional lives. Most of us have a career goal (mission) and a set of principles that guide our behavior (values), but as human beings we are much more. Those who interact with us come to know us by the way we speak and listen, our smarts, our humor, our compassion, our sense of design, and so on. This total package is our personal brand, just as a company's brand is the sum of so many things.

When a company has a strong brand, life is simpler for those who work there. One can look at opportunities or decisions as "on brand" or "off brand." Staying on brand helps clarify the way a company is perceived. Going off brand tends to dilute a company's focus and sow the seeds of confusion.

Because the health of the brand is critical, some business leaders might get nervous when they think about simplifying. They might worry that simplification will diminish the brand, when in fact the opposite is true. When a company simplifies, its brand becomes stronger, more compelling, and more valuable—simply because people will understand and appreciate it more. When a company becomes more complicated, it sends multiple signals that dilute the brand.

This is why Steve Jobs was so focused on building and reinforcing the Apple brand and vigorously opposed any idea that would splinter it. For example, some critics have long argued that Apple's phone business will stagnate without a low-cost option. Steve saw Apple as a premium brand appealing to those who believe that a high-quality, well-designed product is worth a premium price. If Apple were to create that "cheap" phone, it might well increase market share, but it would also dilute its brand. Steve believed that a strong brand is—literally and figuratively—money in the bank.

Defining a brand clearly is one of the simplest rules of marketing and, unsurprisingly, one of the most straightforward rules of simplicity. If you ensure that every action the company takes is "on brand," you remove any confusion about who you are, what you do, and the value you provide. You give customers a clear choice between you and your competition.

Of course, different companies have different ways of expressing their brand. One might stand for something that can be seen in all of its products, such as style, reliability, or innovation. Another might stand for something that's more inside our heads than anything we can touch or feel—or even taste.

Reviving a Brand with Emotion

Pretty much everyone on the planet is familiar with Coca-Cola and Pepsi. But unless you've spent time in the Czech Republic, you probably haven't heard of a soft drink called Kofola. This is a success story rooted in the principles of simplicity, in which Kofola found a way to successfully play David against Coke and Pepsi's Goliath.

Before the 1989 Velvet Revolution in Czechoslovakia, Western soft drink companies didn't exactly get the red-carpet treatment under communist rule. The two big colas were allowed only limited production by a state-owned company operating under a license.

In 1960 a Czechoslovakian company set out to create its own version of Coca-Cola, and Kofola was the result. By the 1970s it had become Czechoslovakia's most popular soft drink, produced in many factories around the country. It was bottled, it was sold on tap—it was a visible part of everyday life across the country.

However, following the revolution, everything changed. With the fall of communism, Western companies were suddenly welcome in the newly christened Czech Republic. Coca-Cola and Pepsi marched right in and the old brands were pushed to the sidelines, including the once-favorite, Kofola. Ultimately Kofola disappeared from shelves entirely.

Many years later, in 1998, Kofola got a new lease on life when Greek immigrant Kostas Samaras bought the rights to the brand, and then bought it outright three years later. By this time Czechs had become enamored with Coke and Pepsi. But Kostas understood that the big brands had never really replaced Kofola, mostly because Kofola had a taste that was quite distinctive.

Though it may look like a cola, Kofola is born of a different recipe, a mix of fourteen vegetable-based flavors. While the difference between Coke and Pepsi is subtle to many, the difference between Kofola and the big-company colas is impossible to miss. The polite way to say it is that Kofola is an acquired taste. Depending on whom you ask, either Kofola is one of the world's greatest refreshments or it's nearly impossible to get past sip number one. Regardless, it still held a place in the hearts of many Czechs.

Thanks to Kostas's entrepreneurial instinct, Kofola returned to the Czech Republic, where it would now go head-to-head with the soda giants. How could such a small company do that? Competing on taste would be a formidable task, but in the Czech Republic Kofola could beat anyone when it came to nostalgia.

Kofola didn't appeal to consumers by being the cool, hip drink of the Coke and Pepsi generations. Rather, it was the taste of people's youth. It was the taste of growing up in Czechoslovakia, being with family, and making friends back in the days when Kofola flowed freely from bottles and taps across the country.

Faced with the challenge of battling the giant cola companies, Kofola built a brand around one simple concept: those warm feelings of nostalgia. Kostas brought back the label designed in 1960 and made nostalgia the backbone of the marketing effort.

Because Kostas communicated the brand personality so well, Kofola became a part of life in the Czech Republic once again. It quickly grew to become a major player among soft drinks and juices, right alongside Coke and Pepsi. The parent company, called the Kofola Group, now employs more than 2,100 people across seven production plants in the Czech Republic, Slovakia, Poland, and Russia.

In 2004 Kostas's son Jannis took over as the CEO of the Kofola Group and the company's growth continued. The brand grew even more powerful, and the clear expression of the brand served as a lure for new customers, as well as new employees who were attracted by the values they shared.

In a competitive marketplace Kofola's brand was a simplifier that made a real difference.

Of Cars and Complexity

Former Apple marketing chief Steve Wilhite's experience in the automotive category actually went far beyond Volkswagen. He led the marketing charge for Nissan and Hyundai as well, so he's very familiar with automobiles and the power of brands.

Wilhite observes that the truly great brands set themselves apart by standing for something special and doing so consistently. They're consistent in the way they express their brand not just from ad to ad but from country to country. This is in contrast to companies that sacrifice consistency in pursuit of some perceived local advantage, portraying the brand in different ways for different audiences.

Companies that sell unique models in specific countries, says Wilhite, seem to believe that the roads in Thailand are different from the roads in China, which are different from the roads in Japan, Germany, and the United States. They develop cars deemed appropriate for the market conditions and customer expectations in each of those markets. Some marketers obviously find a certain cultural or geographic logic to that. Wilhite sees it differently.

> *It's interesting to note that the companies that have consistently been the most profitable, and that have the highest brand value, are the companies that never bought into that philosophy.*

As proof, he points to the behavior of the world's premium automobile brands. The Ferrari you see in Shanghai is no different from the one you see in Beverly Hills, Berlin, or London. And the price you pay reflects the value and clarity that the brand has achieved over time. The same is true of Porsche. Porsche doesn't build a Chinese 911 or an American 911 or a Brazilian 911. It builds a Porsche 911. Likewise, BMW offers the same 3 Series vehicles in different markets around the world. BMW is a brand that has been imbued with meaning, and is effectively marketed as "the ultimate driving machine" everywhere it's sold. In Wilhite's view, BMW is a brand that travels.

Great brands have values that tend to transcend cultures and languages.
They tend to be timeless.

Wilhite points to former Ford CEO Alan Mulally as an example of a leader who had the courage to bring this type of simplicity to a large corporation. Mulally did things that were contrary to common behavior in the auto industry. Wilhite recalls the gist of his message: "One Ford. We're not going to build different cars for different markets. We're going to put our best engineering resources to work. We will build cars like the Ford Focus and the Ford Fusion, which can be sold across all markets and marketed the same way. They will offer the same values, the same characteristics, the same engineering." He used the power of his office to demand that it be so.

There is a real, profound, and sensible need to be culturally sensitive. There are also values that transcend culture. Wilhite stresses that iconic brands find those values, align themselves with those values, and use them to achieve relevance in every geographic location.

> *That's what Apple did with the* Think different *campaign. What difference did it make if Picasso was French or Spanish or American? What difference did it make where Maria Callas, Amelia Earhart, and Jim Henson were born, or where these people made their contributions? All of these people made contributions that were inspirational. They changed the world—not just their native country. And so the Apple brand transcends culture.*

This type of brand clarity doesn't always come easily. Even within the companies that transcend culture, there is often debate about how the brand should be expressed in different locales. Wilhite reveals that even though Steve Jobs was clear about what he wanted to do with the *Think different* campaign, some parts of Apple's global marketing organization disagreed with his thinking.

On occasion, Apple staff in different countries wanted to "do their own thing" in their specific region. In Japan, for example, the local Apple office feared running product ads with all the white space that defined Apple's aesthetic at the time. They put together a thick portfolio of successful Japanese campaigns to prove their point that Japanese customers would be put off by Apple's style. In such instances, Wilhite says it was his job to say no. He would explain the strategy to these people and then invite them to celebrate and embrace it.

> *The Apple brand wasn't about to change. This was who we were as a company. I'd say to them, "So keep taking your best shot, but you're really wasting your time. And at some point someone is going to say, 'You know what, you just don't get it. You're fired.'"*

Everyone who has worked for a global company understands that as much as you'd like to be nice about it, there can be no compromise on the things of supreme importance. In the world of Steve Jobs, the brand was something to be cherished and nurtured, never diminished. It has always been a vital part of Apple's simplicity, serving as a guiding light for so many key decisions.

Meeting the Brand Face-to-Face

Creating a physical Apple Store was a pivotal moment in the company's history. Inside the Apple Store, customers would for the first time have direct personal contact with the Apple brand. The challenge was to design a retail environment that communicated the company's values, so that the very act of entering the store would give one a sense of Apple.

Prior to the creation of the Apple Stores, the only way for people to experience the products was to visit an authorized reseller, where Apple might be just one of many brands carried. Years earlier, with some fanfare, Apple had pursued a store-within-a-store model at now-defunct CompUSA, but that experiment had fizzled. Salespeople were simply not invested in Apple. Their knowledge of Apple products wasn't particularly deep. They'd just as happily sell a customer a PC instead of a Mac.

A chain of Apple-owned stores would change all that forever. Finally new customers and loyal customers could have a personal relationship with the brand and its emphasis on innovation, design, and simplicity. Ron Johnson talks about those early days of debates and fine-tuning of the Apple Store's brand leading up to the opening of the first Apple Store in 2001:

> *I remember telling Steve Jobs when we started: Be prepared. Right now people see Apple as a product—but in the stores people's impression of Apple will be a place. Remember, we only had 3 percent market share back then. The physical store would be how we reached out to the other 97 percent, and the store would be their first impression of Apple—every bit as important as the products themselves.*

Where does one even begin when undertaking such a project? Ron explains that two decisions had to be made before any actual work could begin: How big would the stores be and where would they be?

> *I asked Steve how big the product line is, and he said, "This big." He was pointing to the conference room table, which could easily hold Apple's entire product line. And I said, "How big is the brand? Is it as big as Gap?" He said, "Bigger."*

Ron's point of view was that if Apple's stores weren't physically at least as big as Gap's, comparatively the brand would feel smaller. That's just the way people tend to judge things—a small store feels more like a boutique.

After much discussion, it was decided that the physical Apple Store would be approximately the size of a typical Gap store. That one decision led directly to other decisions, like how much rent to pay and how much revenue the stores needed to generate. The size of the store was the starting point for every discussion about how the stores would be set up and how they would feel to those who walked through the doors.

Steve approached the Apple Store like it was the latest Apple product, pouring his energy into the first version, hoping to shake up the category. But what Ron was developing wasn't really a product at all—it was an experience. Those who entered the Apple Store would become immersed in the brand.

This thinking led us to build a store based around an experience that is so much greater than the products. Most retail stores are basically designed to house a product line. They're just a warehouse for products. We were designing a showcase where people could understand how our products fit into their lives.

A prototype store was built in a secret location, and that's where Ron and his team experimented with different building materials, fixtures, and layouts. Steve and Ron would visit the store together once a week. At that time the retail team would share what was new, and Steve would react. It was a long period of trying things out to come up with the most compelling combination of elements.

Once that first store was designed, Steve's attitude was "Now go build a bunch of stores." He didn't have to obsess over every new store, because he knew they'd all be built to the high standard of the first—the manifestation of the Apple brand. That would free him to concentrate on the next big project, Ron said.

Steve spent all his time on a few things. And he liked to focus on one thing at a time. When Apple set out to build a phone, he'd concentrate on the phone. He would spend whatever time it took to get it right. Many companies enter a variety of categories with a variety of products, but Steve just went deep on one at a time. He was almost binary that way—"We'll do this first, and then we'll do that next." He stayed excep-tionally focused.

The Apple Store experience feels natural to many of us today. It has an Apple-esque atmosphere with its open spaces and uncluttered displays. De-signed this way, it builds upon the perception of the brand that most people already have—and adds a human element with a large, knowledgeable, and helpful staff.

Reverence for the brand had always been a part of the Steve Jobs phi-losophy. In *Insanely Simple* I talked about Steve's concept of "the brand bank." He believed that every positive experience a customer had with the company (a compelling ad, a beautiful product, high-quality packaging, a wonderful in-store experience, etc.) was a deposit in the bank, and every bad moment (a flawed product, negative press, a bad ad, an unpleasant ser-vice experience, etc.) was a withdrawal from the bank. Looking at the brand this way, Steve felt it was important to take advantage of every opportunity to make a deposit in the brand bank, because a high balance meant Apple was winning customers' hearts. That high balance would not only keep customers loyal but would also build a cushion to help the company with-stand any unexpected negative publicity that might occur in the future.

The Apple Stores represented a massive opportunity to add to the Apple brand bank.

Deepening the Brand, Not Cheapening the Brand

Though former marketing chief Steve Wilhite worked at Apple before the Apple Stores were conceived, he witnessed Jobs's deep commitment to the brand and how it helped simplify decisions.

Wilhite says he felt like the keeper of the sacred flame. It was his job not only to elevate the Apple brand when possible but also to protect it from damage when he sensed trouble. Part of his responsibility was to keep everyone on the same page in support of the brand, which required constant vigilance.

As an example, Wilhite tells the story of an Apple sales executive who appeared in his office one day in 1998, totally excited after being approached by Pepsi. Pepsi was planning to spend $30 million in broadcast media for a consumer giveaway campaign and was prepared to purchase three thousand iMacs to award as prizes. Pepsi would put the image of the iMac on every can, six-pack, and carton it sold; it would feature the computer on big displays in convenience stores and cover North America with its "Buy a Pepsi, Win an iMac" campaign.

At that time the iMac was just taking off as Apple's hot new product, and the company's recovery was only beginning. The idea of selling three thousand computers to Pepsi in one swoop was pretty darn tempting. The sales executive was giddy at the prospect, so he was taken aback when Wilhite gave him a quick and resounding "no."

> *He looked at me as if I were from Mars. So I explained to him, "What's happening here is that Pepsi wants to use our brand equity, our product, as the prize behind door number three to help them sell more of their sugar water. We move three thousand iMacs, but we don't get to tell anybody who we are, what we stand for, or why it matters. We don't get to explain our value proposition in any way. We don't get to say we're the best computer for the Internet, best computer for design, nothing. We're just a gift that you might get if you happen to buy the lucky can of Pepsi. So we're not going to do this."*

That put a damper on Mr. Salesman's shot at glory. Believing that Wilhite was dismissing a huge marketing opportunity, he went straight to Jobs. Jobs not only backed Wilhite up but later thanked him for protecting the brand.

> *I doubt there are many CEOs who would have declined the media exposure and revenue from the sale of three thousand computers at a time when we had just borrowed $150 million from Microsoft and were trying to reestablish our brand.*

This is the kind of thinking that for many years has kept Apple perched at or near the top of the charts tracking the world's most valuable brands. When the brand remains top of mind, even thorny decisions become simpler.

Wilhite says that the number one reason he accepted the marketing position with Apple was that he wanted to work for a company that shared his belief in the power of a brand—and there was no doubt where Jobs stood on that issue. In his prehiring conversations it was clear that Jobs appreciated the role of marketing in enhancing the brand, crystallizing customers' perceptions, and unifying different parts of the company.

He also understood that the brand must be nurtured and grown over time.

Consistency Is a Brand's Best Friend

Wilhite's stories about the brand brought to mind an experience I had on the agency side during the same period. It was our job to create advertising that not only announced the latest products but also helped make deposits in the Apple brand bank.

The goal of every creative person in advertising is to make something new and never get stuck in a box. However, when you work with a brand like Apple, that desire can put you between a rock and a hard place. You want to refresh the brand in unexpected ways, but when it comes to look and feel, you're expected to play within the sandbox that's been established. To do otherwise could harm the brand.

At one point we welcomed a new art director to the agency's Apple team. His claim to fame was the outstanding work he'd been doing for another iconic brand that was much admired in the creative community. He was a talented man, a good guy, and we were confident that he was the right person for the job.

In about six months he was gone.

What happened was that our new hire didn't appreciate the equity

Apple had built up in its brand over the years. In his desire to think outside the box, he designed ads that were busy and unstructured as opposed to simple and elegant, as would have been consistent with the Apple brand. He didn't even use the Apple typeface. Instead he pushed for handwritten headlines scratched across the page.

He wasn't just tossing aside the rules—he was tossing aside the equity Apple had lovingly nurtured over many years. To someone like Steve Jobs his work conjured the unsettling feeling of "creativity for creativity's sake" as opposed to creativity in service of the brand.

Again, the culture defended itself against an intruder. The art director quickly felt out of place working on the business when his ideas were spurned—sometimes not so gently—and returned to his prior job, where he felt more appreciated.

The truth is, successful brands absolutely do evolve, often in surprising and wonderful new directions. But they do not lightly toss aside identifying characteristics that help customers identify with the brand. These elements can include graphic design, typography, or simply an attitude.

"Consistency" is one of those words that can be insult or praise. On the negative side, one can quote Ralph Waldo Emerson, who said, "With consistency, a great soul has simply nothing to do. He may as well concern himself with his shadow on the wall."

However, consistency can be an ally of simplicity and creativity alike. In the case of Apple's marketing, consistency has been a tremendous simplifier, allowing the company to speak with a familiar tone yet still have room to evolve. Steve Wilhite articulates this well.

> *Apple found that space and tone that allowed it to do wonderful work. It continues to be fresh and relevant yet uniquely Apple. If I look at the arc of work from* Think different *through some of the iPhone and iPad work, it all hangs together as a single brand. There have been highs and lows, but the arc of the story is consistent. That makes the brand even stronger over time.*

Though Apple's ads have felt consistent for decades, they've evolved in some striking ways, just as the company's products have. That's because consistency doesn't just give customers a familiar way to connect. It creates a path that allows the brand to evolve sensibly.

Over in Australia I found an unusual example of a financial brand that evolved over time—including several years of hibernation.

Even a Sleeping Brand Has Power

Victoria is Australia's second-biggest state, home to the country's second-biggest city, Melbourne. It was here that a series of moves within the banking industry demonstrated how being true to a brand can create a simpler business model.

This story involves three banking brands that have had a presence in Victoria: Westpac Bank (one of Australia's biggest, as we saw in chapter 3), St.George Bank (doing business across several states), and Bank of Melbourne (a Victorian bank).

Westpac's parent, the Westpac Group, acquired Bank of Melbourne in 1997 and quickly renamed its branches Westpac Bank, making the Bank of Melbourne brand but a memory. Years later, after a merger, St.George Bank also became a part of the Westpac Group. By 2011 Westpac's presence in Victoria consisted entirely of St.George and Westpac branches—but business wasn't exactly booming.

That's when Scott Tanner arrived at Westpac and was given the task of creating a profitable banking business in Victoria. His belief in the power of simplicity helped him create a major success story in the Australian banking sector. Says Scott:

> In my prior job, with the consultancy Bain & Company, I was always banging on about simplicity. We had a section called the "complexity reduction group." For me that was the core of the problem: we couldn't even put a simple name to it. It's hard to sell the idea of simplicity when even your name is complicated.

Scott brought that challenger attitude to Westpac and applied it to his immediate task. He recognized that in the busy Victorian marketplace, any new bank would face serious competition.

If you want to get "cut-through" in a busy world, you must have a simple, unifying idea that informs the way you do business. That gives you focus and a coherent, consistent story.

As Scott and his team searched for that unifying idea, they became fascinated with the power of a local brand. While national and global banks offer size and strength, many customers believe that a local brand better understands their lives and needs, because it's more accessible and more involved in the community. Around the world, 25 to 45 percent of consumers and businesses were using a regional bank, yet in Victoria that number was only 13 percent.

That gap presented a huge opportunity. Why would fewer Victorians do business with a local bank? Logic said there must be an unmet need. And so "local" became the core idea for the new bank, and the foundation for the "coherent, consistent" story Scott was seeking.

This thinking led directly to the resurrection of the Bank of Melbourne brand. A bank dedicated to Victoria had the potential to resonate with locals, appealing to their pride in the state's internationally celebrated lifestyle and business environment.

Scott believes that when local banks go national, both customers and staff begin to lose emotional attachment. Being deeply rooted in the local community would give Bank of Melbourne the opportunity to build new bonds and generate positive word of mouth. That's exactly what happened. The bank's relaunch became a visible success from day one.

Scott felt it was important to make the story about the future and not about the brand's legacy. He wanted to focus on creating a niche that the bank would be known for. He absolutely did not want to be all things to all people, because that's exactly what most banks do.

Bank of Melbourne would focus on only three things: home financing, starting or growing a business, and preparing for retirement. Though he was reviving a brand from the past, Scott was essentially bringing a new company to life. That was a liberating thing, he says.

> *Being a start-up has given us the freedom that other banks don't have. Because we're simpler and more focused, we get more cut-through in a competitive industry. We didn't have a legacy to protect. We could focus on building the bank we wanted to have in the future.*

Launching a new brand built on the idea of the "local bank" led to some interesting and bold decisions. One big change was the physical layout of the bank branches. Rather than design branches for transactions—which most people take care of today through personal technology—branches were designed to promote conversations. If you aim to have pleasant, productive conversations, says Scott, it's probably best if one party isn't set up in a cage or sitting behind bulletproof glass.

So he adopted a European model that's all about interaction. Staff is out on the floor, talking with customers face-to-face. If need be, they can sit down with a customer at a computer to solve problems or offer advice.

In redesigning the customer experience to fit the brand, Scott also had to rethink his hiring criteria. After all, people who are comfortable sitting in a teller's cage wouldn't necessarily feel comfortable interacting with customers on the floor. As a result, 70 percent of the bank's customer-service staff has been hired from outside the banking industry.

> *The last thing I wanted to do was to only hire people from other banks. I wanted to build a team that actually* likes *people and loves customer service. We recruited people from the local community for each branch because they understood the language and culture of their local area. It's another example of taking that single, unifying idea and applying it to everything we do.*

Where else did this simple brand idea lead? Directly to the customer-service call center. Scott felt that Bank of Melbourne couldn't truly be a local bank unless it had a local call center, so he built one in central Melbourne. Now, instead of being transferred to another country, calls are handled by locals who are far better equipped to engage with customers and appreciate their issues.

The physical change to the bank's branches was accomplished with impressive speed. One Friday in 2011 doors closed on the St.George branches, and over the weekend the signage, collateral, and office layout became 100 percent Bank of Melbourne. At the opening hour on Monday morning, it was a brand-new bank.

The change on that weekend was a lightbulb moment for everyone involved. It was extraordinary. Engagement and morale skyrocketed because there was a tangible sense of doing things differently. We'd built a team that was passionate about making a sustainable contribution to Victorians and local communities. This was their bank too.

Three elements underpin the pride that Victorians feel about Melbourne, even if they live outside the city, and the bank has forged links with all three. It partners with the Melbourne Cricket Ground, the city's favorite sports arena. It's involved with Melbourne's vibrant food and wine industry, as well as local arts and cultural institutions. And, at the grassroots level, every branch is encouraged to get out into its neighborhood and support small, local organizations. Since 2013 the bank has also contributed more than a million dollars to community-based organizations from its own charitable program.

Bank of Melbourne doesn't make a lot of noise about its community involvement. Scott believes it's more about the passion of the branch employees who invest their time, talent, and energy. This interaction deepens relationships and has an impact on people's lives.

Under Scott's leadership the bank's clarity and purpose have fueled its success. The original footprint of thirty-four branches has now expanded to more than a hundred. The original workforce of three hundred has grown to more than twelve hundred.

A clear and consistent brand is a powerful engine for growth.

Simplicity Is Always On Brand

Despite what some rating organizations might lead you to believe, a brand isn't quite so easy to quantify. That's because, as we've seen, perceptions of the brand are influenced by many different factors.

Some leaders have an intuitive sense about their brand, which helps them guide and protect it. In a product or marketing meeting, they might ponder a new idea before coming to the conclusion that "it's just not us." That's their way of saying the idea is off brand. In other words, it would either fail to reinforce the brand, or, even worse, diminish it.

A strong brand has a simplifying effect for the company's leaders, employees, and customers alike. For those on the inside, it helps point to the right direction when certain decisions are made. For those on the outside, it's how they "know" the company—it shapes the way they perceive it and how they talk about it to others.

For all of these reasons, leaders who believe in the power of simplicity are typically unbending about the need to nourish their brand. And every time they do so it's another deposit in the brand bank.

Chapter 6
Simplicity Fits All Sizes

It's an immutable law of nature: Small companies operate more simply than big ones. After all, complexities aren't terribly difficult to deal with when your company consists of twenty people working in a loft. Small companies have the benefit of less hierarchy, more focus, smaller product lines, and better communication.

But even if a big company can't be totally simple, it absolutely can be *simpler*—and the gains to be made from simplification are without limit. In fact, some of the best lessons in simplicity come from companies that have grappled with complexity on a grand scale. I'm talking about banks, telecommunication companies, multinationals, and many other businesses that employ thousands of people across multiple offices.

However simple those companies may have been at birth, over time "things get complicated." Product lines expand, workforces grow, hierarchies are formalized, processes proliferate, and suddenly the company that once seemed so beautifully focused is struggling to keep morale high and customers happy.

What can a big company do to counter the forces of complexity, which in some cases have been doing damage for years or even decades? Many of those interviewed for this book took a similar and logical approach: They put themselves in the shoes of the customer.

By trusting the instincts they'd gained through years of experience and seeing their business from the customer's point of view, they were able to bring refreshing simplicity to the way their big business operates. Equally important, they had no problem ruffling feathers in the name of simplification. Leaders with a true passion for simplicity are willing to challenge processes and policies that seem arbitrary or burdensome or fly in the face of simple logic.

Some big companies have never had to face a crisis of complexity. They're the ones who embraced simplicity early on and built it into their culture. For them, the challenge was to avoid complacency. As they grew into big companies, they were mindful of the threat and made an effort to ensure that complexity did not take root.

Whether you're trying to simplify a complicated organization or inoculate a growing company against complexity, you'll likely gain valuable insights from the leaders who've been on the front lines.

Fixing Apple the "Simple, Boneheaded Way"

In *Insanely Simple* I defined simplicity as the combination of brains and common sense. I based that largely on what I had observed in the actions of Steve Jobs in turning Apple into what it is today.

True, many of Steve's best-known decisions were bold and had world-changing effects. But in guiding the development of new products and marketing plans week to week, many of his decisions were obvious and logical. There were times I felt that common sense—or, more accurately, the ability to *act* on common sense—was Steve's greatest strength.

What Steve did to simplify Apple upon his return in 1997 could be the "proof of concept" your company needs before it commits to simplification. It's proof that even a giant company mired in complexity can be turned around in a most dramatic fashion.

One of Steve's first official acts upon returning was to boot previous CEO Gil Amelio's ad agency and rehire his old ad team at TBWA\Chiat\ Day. Simultaneously he shuffled off most of the senior marketing team he'd inherited from Amelio and appointed a new marketing leader, Allen Olivo.

Allen had worked at Apple for a number of years before Steve returned, so he has an interesting perspective on how Steve went about transforming the company. I particularly enjoyed the way he commented, with a wink, that Steve revived Apple "the simple, boneheaded way." Especially since Steve was about as far from boneheaded as a human being can get. Allen was referring to the fact that Steve approached the restructuring of Apple in a way that was functionally driven and refreshingly simple. He remembers:

> It was very clear who was responsible for what. "Don't worry about her job, because I'm going to worry about her job. If she's not doing her job, I will fire her. You worry about your job—because I'm going to worry about your job too."
>
> I think the reason Steve took this fundamentally functional, simple approach was that it was the only way he could keep straight in his head who was doing what.

We've already talked about Steve's desire to hire only the most brilliant people. Not only did he have an innate talent for finding these people, but he was also very good at making room for them. In his special way with words, Steve referred to that process as "firing the bozos."

Basically, upon his return Steve worked hard to remove eleven years' worth of cobwebs in the Apple organization. He was put off by big-company organizational structures and therefore sought to streamline the complicated management hierarchy at an Apple that was once again under his control. There would be no committees and no complex approval processes. He would restore the entrepreneurial spirit and celebrate fresh thinking.

Steve's goal was to get Apple back in the innovation business. To do that, he'd need people who were capable of innovating in the most eye-opening ways. You might be familiar with what happened next, but it can't be ignored in any book examining the value of simplification.

Taking stock of what he had to work with, Steve visited the hidden lair of Apple's design group. There he met Jony Ive and his team, who were basically fed up with Apple's lack of interest in breakthrough design and ready to abandon ship. Under Amelio's leadership, design had fallen down in the list of Apple's priorities. Still dreaming of winning in the corporate environment, the Amelio administration had been wary of any approach that might turn off the business crowd. Risky design was just . . . too risky.

Steve assured Jony that design would play a major role in the reinvented Apple and persuaded him to stick around. Not a bad career move for Jony, as it turned out.

The difference-maker for Apple's future was that Steve had the instinct to empower Jony and his team. He made sure there was a seat at the executive table for those who personified the company's spirit of innovation—a spirit that had eroded over the years. This was Steve's way of creating a visible focus for a company that had been wandering. In one swoop, it reaffirmed Apple's mission, culture, and values.

Had Steve not empowered Jony, Apple might never have recovered as it did. In this story is a good lesson for any company in a state of stagnation: It's entirely possible that the answer to the company's problem is already on the payroll. As Steve demonstrated, reassessing priorities and empowering the right people can go a long way in reenergizing an organization.

Next, Steve went about removing the distractions so Apple could regain its intense focus. Distraction number one was Apple's lawsuit against Microsoft alleging that Windows on the PC platform violated Apple's patents for the Macintosh interface. The litigation had dragged on for years. Steve negotiated a truce with Bill Gates, dropping the suit in exchange for Microsoft's $150 million investment in Apple and its pledge to support Microsoft Office on the Mac platform for the next five years. That promise brought some security to those who might consider a Macintosh computer. It helped Microsoft as well, as it was facing legal actions for monopolistic behaviors.

Here was proof that Microsoft was actively supporting a platform beyond PCs.

Many Apple fans were upset that Steve would reconcile with "the enemy." But at Macworld Boston in 1997, Steve countered by saying, "We have to let go of this notion that for Apple to win, Microsoft has to lose. We have to embrace the notion that for Apple to win, Apple has to do a really good job. And if others are going to help us, that's great." By settling this dispute Steve brought focus back to the organization.

Next Steve set his sights on the company's products. When he retook the throne in Cupertino, Apple's reputation for innovation and quality had been seriously tarnished. The company was bleeding money with a line of over twenty distinct products (laptops, desktops, Newtons, printers, scanners, cameras, etc.), each requiring a budget for R&D and marketing. It had also licensed other manufacturers to put the Macintosh OS in a variety of non-Apple machines. There was much here to simplify.

At the very same event where he unveiled the iMac in 1998, Steve announced that he was effectively killing Apple's entire product line (except for two computer models). I can find no example of any company ever doing such a thing before.

Instead of making so many different products, Apple would now make only four—home and pro versions of a desktop and a laptop. Cutting the number of products would have two effects. First, it would end the splintering of resources necessary to support so many products. Second, it would launch a whole new product philosophy at Apple. No longer would Apple make products simply to have a presence in a certain category. From that day forward, every Apple product would be "best in class" or the company simply would not participate.

With this radical redefining of the product line, Steve gave birth to the philosophy that still guides Apple to this day. In simpler terms, it's the pursuit of quality over quantity. Steve's bold decision enabled the company to survive financially and begin building its modern reputation for innovation, design, reliability, and craftsmanship. These are the things that would set Apple apart from competitors and help build a brand that justifies a premium price.

Steve's new direction proved one of simplicity's boldest claims: A company can excel by doing fewer things better.

As he attacked the product line, Steve also attacked Apple's internal organization. He collapsed the hierarchy and prioritized ideas over processes. Less than a year after his return, Steve assessed the company's restructuring in a 1998 interview with *BusinessWeek**. He said, "The organization is clean and simple to understand, and very accountable. Everything just got simpler." He summed it up by identifying his mantras: "Focus and simplicity."

There is something about crisis and impending doom that can spur a company to action, as happened at Apple. For the sake of your health, however, I recommend simplifying before you get to that point.

But before we exit crisis mode, let's take a look at another company that faced an Apple-like turning point—and also had the benefit of a leader with a talent for simplification.

Simplicity Remakes a Financial Powerhouse

Earlier we heard from Ted Chung, who leads Hyundai Card in South Korea.

With Hyundai Card being one of that nation's leading credit card companies, I approached my conversation with Ted expecting him to be a master of finance. Though he certainly knows his industry inside and out, what makes Ted's story even more impressive is that he did *not* come from the world of finance. Despite that "shortcoming"—or perhaps because of it—he's managed to turn Hyundai Card into a remarkable success story.

Ted started as CEO of Hyundai Motor Group's Mexican operations, becoming the leader of a factory of 2,500 workers that had been losing

---

* *BusinessWeek,* "Steve Jobs: There's Sanity Returning," May 25, 1998, interview with *Business-Week* correspondent Andy Reinhardt, http://www.businessweek.com/1998/21/b3579165.htm.

money for ten years. Under Ted's leadership that factory turned around within three years to achieve the highest profitability within the Hyundai family of companies.

That success paved the way for Ted's move to Seoul, where he would lead the three financial divisions of Hyundai to profitability. However, it was only when he made the move that he came to understand the full magnitude of the losses his companies were facing. Projections showed that his three companies together could lose up to $2 billion that year. Somehow, Ted saw the silver lining in that terrifying number.

> *My wife thought my reaction was quite odd. I was actually excited to learn that my companies might lose $2 billion that year.*

Rather than being intimidated by that number, Ted saw this as the business opportunity of a lifetime. As we know, turning failure into success is one of the most thrilling business experiences—and turning *huge* failure into success is even more exciting.

Ted came to better appreciate the uniqueness of Hyundai Card within the Hyundai family. There were about sixty other Hyundai companies, most making things like cars and engines. Hyundai Card was different in that it provided consumers with financial products that went beyond automobile ownership. There was plenty of potential for the company to play a major role in the lives of people and businesses.

But how would Ted even start to set the company on a path toward profitability? He took a few months to study the company and introduce himself to his employees in the most honest way he could, by telling them, "I don't know too much about the credit card business, but I am ready to fix this. Just trust me."

Though many have an instinctive fear of trusting anyone who says "Trust me," Ted found a way to deliver. The more he talked to people about the company's direction, the more he realized that something important was missing. Employees had no sense of mission and therefore nothing to be passionate about. What they needed was a central focus—something that would symbolize the company's mission and galvanize different groups in pursuit of the common goal. What they needed, as Ted describes it, was a "front line."

> *Our employees didn't know who the enemy was, and they had no target to aim for. They were generally unmotivated and feeling empty. To start the change process, I had to create a single front line.*

One night around eight o'clock, when the building was mostly empty, Ted took a walk around the office. He happened upon four men working in a small office and struck up a conversation. He asked what they were doing, and they replied that they were working on a new credit card.

Impressed by their willingness to work into the night, Ted ran out to Starbucks, brought back a cup of coffee for each, and asked to hear more. They told Ted they were working on revitalizing a cash-back card to allow customers who bought a Hyundai or Kia car to get up to five hundred dollars in cash back *before* they made purchases. Subsequent purchases would then be credited toward that amount, and then they could earn more cash back with more purchases. Ted was impressed. This, he felt, was the front line he was looking for. The credit card, called the M Card, offered something different, and that difference was to represent the new spirit at Hyundai Card.

The company was already set to invest $500,000 in this project. Ted raised that figure to $50 *million*. If this was to become the single focus of the company, he wanted to do an amazing job with it. "Let's make it real huge big," said Ted, amping up his adjectives along with his investment.

> *I came here in January when the company was in crisis. Just months later I launched this new M credit card and increased the budget. Many people said I was crazy. If we're facing a possible loss of $2 billion, how can we spend another $50 million? I said, "What's the difference between losing $2 billion and $2 billion plus $50 million? We're already dead."*

In making this investment, Ted's goal was to create a positive public image for Hyundai Card while also sending a strong message to his employees.

This is our new product and we will devote our life to this product. This is the front line. Every employee, in every corner of this company, needs to focus on this. If we are successful, our future is bright.

This effort unified the company in ways it had never been before. It helped turn a splintered company into a single-minded organization, everyone marching in sync toward the new goal.

This was only the start. Ted knew that he couldn't create a change of magnitude if the employees were fearful. To negate apprehension and ward off morale problems, he surprised the entire workforce by giving everyone a 10 percent raise.

He also recruited some unusual talent to help in the company's revival. Rather than seeking out the smartest credit card experts, Ted focused on hiring brilliant people from different industries, those who could spark new ways of thinking at Hyundai Card.

There's an echo of Steve Jobs in this approach. In the 1996 PBS production *Triumph of the Nerds,* Steve says, "I think part of what made the Macintosh great was that the people working on it were musicians and poets and artists and zoologists and historians—who also happened to be the best computer scientists in the world."

Ted felt that it wouldn't be difficult to educate smart, creative people about the credit card business and that the rewards of bringing in talented people from other industries would far outweigh the need for a bit of education up front. Many of those he hired were young. His top lieutenant was the ripe old age of thirty-three.

He also put together a six-person leadership team, which would later expand to twelve. Ultimately, more than half of Ted's leadership team was made up of industry outsiders. This was the group that would help Hyundai choose an innovative path toward recovery and growth. Every week the team would meet for two hours to discuss the challenges and initiatives they would tackle in the upcoming week.

Ted has received quite a bit of business press for transforming a company so deep in the red to one of the most profitable and popular companies in South Korea. He attributes much of his success to the power of simplicity. Success came from instilling a sense of mission in the workforce by identifying a front line that would bring people together and from empowering those with the right talent—even if they weren't experts in the business.

The M Card was launched in 2003, and in one year's time it boasted one million members. Within four years it was the best-selling credit card in South Korea, with a membership of five million.

The extraordinary success of the M Card allowed Hyundai Card to overcome its deep financial crisis. It also opened the company's eyes to the possibilities ahead. A new way of working would lead to many more successes in the coming years.

Ted did not aim to make all of his changes from the start, even though the company was clearly in a state of failure. He made a few critical changes quickly and then continued to institute new policies every month or two as fresh thinking and strategies emerged from the regular leadership team meetings.

While crises such as those faced by Ted Chung are one impetus for simplification, a far better reason is that simplification is just good business. Especially when your company is part of an industry long known for complexity.

Can a Big Bank Really Get Simpler?

Big banks have historically faced an uphill battle to win the hearts of consumers. Most people aren't inclined to have warm and fuzzy thoughts about large financial institutions. After all, much of their experience with banking over the years has required them to deal with confusing choices, unbending rules, and rising fees.

The story of Westpac Bank in Australia demonstrates how simplicity can take root in the most challenging environment and produce compelling results.

CEO Brian Hartzer honed his ideas on simplification as the CEO of UK Retail and Wealth Management at Royal Bank of Scotland. At the time, RBS was in terrible shape, not unlike Apple in the late 1990s. Brian went about changing its business with simplicity as his theme. He took a fresh look at the bank's products, services, call centers, and more.

It was about focusing on what we know, the core of what we do, and making sure we do it well. That not only reduced costs and drove up revenue, it reduced some of the risks—because more complexity and more variation equal more opportunities to screw things up.

Westpac was in good financial health when Brian joined in 2012. Still, the world was changing fast with the rise of technology and, following the global financial crisis, the bank had to deal with regulatory and societal changes as well. Add to that some serious competition in the world of Australian banking, and Brian faced a bevy of major challenges.

He quickly noticed two potential obstacles to the bank's ongoing success: the complexity of its offerings and a lack of strategic clarity in its positioning. Brian's method of getting to a simpler place was to "swim upstream."

A lot of people talk about the complexity of a bank's technology platform and operations. But when you swim upstream from that, what you find is the original product set. Pure and simple. You come to realize that almost all of the complexity in the bank's systems, processes, policies, and so on are actually just a downstream effect. They're the result of an environment that has sought, over time, to add features and functionality to products or to add new products to go after a perceived market opportunity.

Brian observes that this type of creeping complexity is common in big organizations. He sees it happening in banks because the product managers typically sit in a head office, far away from the people who are actually working with customers.

These product managers, who often come from a marketing background, tend to see the bank's products as packaged goods—almost as if they're selling soap. When tasked with increasing market share or generating new profits, Brian says that they reach into the same tool kit they've always used.

> *They run an ad campaign, or change pricing, or widen margins, or cut costs, or create new products with features they'd been missing. It's like, "When all I have is a hammer, everything looks like a nail."*

Because they are removed from the sales force, product managers can't see how their actions might actually be hampering the sales force's job. Over time the products become so complicated they're more difficult to explain to customers. Even worse, they become confusing to the sales force itself.

Brian took action to arm the frontline sales staff with tools and products that were easy to grasp for employees and customers alike. In his estimation this kind of clarity not only makes business better but also makes business more profitable.

> *My view is that a simpler product set actually makes your staff more competent and your customers more open. Therefore, fewer products should actually help with revenue generation as well.*

Simplifying business in this way also brings welcome benefits to banking in terms of risk and regulations. When processes become simpler, fewer mistakes are made—and fewer mistakes translates directly to happier regulators and less time wasted.

To me, simplicity in financial services is a win-win-win-win-win—across revenue, costs, and risk.

Technically I count only three wins there, but we'll let Brian's enthusiasm carry the day, because for a bank those are three very large wins.

Simplifying the product set wasn't actually a difficult idea to sell to the company. In a complex environment like a bank, a move toward simplicity gets instant support. It's like motherhood, says Brian—everyone's in favor.

Brian also talks about the power of words to simplify a big organization. This is something I wrote about at length in *Insanely Simple*; Apple has amplified its success through its ability to leverage simple, powerful, and memorable words.

As part of his effort to improve the organization, Brian conducted an exercise in which he asked his staff to imagine the future of the Westpac customer experience. His idea was that if they could articulate a vision, they would have a more definitive goal to work toward.

My teams came up with specific ideas of things they wanted to create, which were fabulous. As I sat there trying to organize that into some sort of logical structure, the phrase "service revolution" came up.

Brian found that this phrase had extraordinary power within the organization. It not only described what he wanted to create but also galvanized the staff, inspiring them to invent ways to turn the idea into reality.

The power of words should never be forgotten in the effort to simplify. You don't want to reduce important issues to nursery rhymes, but carefully crafted words can truly align people in a quest. In my advertising life the best test has always been "Does it make a good T-shirt?" If people will wear those words with pride and those words point everyone toward a common goal, you know you've done a good job.

Another term that has played a big part in Brian's simplification, and would look fabulous on a T-shirt, is "heroic bankers." The phrase was tossed out in a meeting by one of his team members. It struck a chord in the room because it was such an unexpected way to describe a banker.

If people outside the industry were to hear that phrase, they'd probably have a nice giggle, admits Brian. But the impact of these words among the bank's workforce has been huge.

> *When I tell the staff I want them to be heroic bankers in the eyes of their customers, they're no longer just service providers. If they do their jobs well, they'll be heroes to their customers—because they'll help customers create a better financial future, solve a scary financial issue, own the home they dreamed of, be secure in their retirement, solve problems, and so on. So now they ask themselves, "What would it take to be a hero in the eyes of my customers?"*

To bring that phrase to life, Brian had to hire the right kind of people. He had to ensure that they received the proper training so they could be empowered to make decisions on the spot. The staff would need to feel a sense of urgency on behalf of their customers and be rewarded for overcoming obstacles.

> *The phrase "heroic banker" can be expanded into a pyramid of actions that can be taken to drive positive change. That one simple idea has led to a really clear set of actions.*

In such a big organization, across so many offices, it's not easy to get everyone on the same page. Yet that simple phrase spread through the company like wildfire, to the point where Brian started to receive emails from people saying, "I've got this great heroic banker story. . . ."

When we spoke, he'd recently received an email about a Westpac employee who responded to an emergency situation, driving a customer to the hospital with his seriously ill wife and staying with the couple to make sure the woman was treated well. Though this was a highly unusual situation having little to do with banking, it certainly gave dimension to the term "heroic banker." It demonstrated a willingness to take extraordinary measures to help a customer.

Another email described heroics in a business sense. A customer was hosting a fund-raiser on a Sunday and didn't think to arrange for a credit card terminal until the Friday before. Unfortunately, the bank's policy made it impossible to get a terminal that quickly. Apprised of the situation, the Westpac branch manager leaped into action. He tracked down those who could make an exception to the rule and succeeded in procuring the terminal. Further, he delivered it personally, enabling the customer to raise $35,000 for the worthy cause.

Brian was able to tell his staff that this man became a hero in the eyes of this customer. He went beyond the call, took specific actions, and performed a service that meant the world to a customer. People get that.

The idea of the heroic banker touched off an enthusiastic movement within the bank and proved again how a simple set of words can power a movement to simplify.

Honestly, I'm amazed how the use of these phrases has taken off. Just one hour ago I was in a meeting with our risk team, and they were showing how all their current projects line up with the principles of the service revolution. The risk team! When simplicity evolves into language, it's a really powerful thing.

At Westpac Bank, Brian is instilling simplicity into an existing large organization. He's swimming upstream to try to recapture some of the simplicity that's been lost and taking action to give teams more focus.

Now let's look at a small company that grew to large proportions yet stubbornly held on to its simplicity. Far from the world of numbers and processes, this company is built purely on creativity.

Simplicity Is Controlled Growth

Blue Man Group is not only a unique brand of entertainment, it's a company with a fascinating business story offering an unusual example of the power of simplicity.

The act began with three street performers in 1987 and has since grown to a company of nearly six hundred employees. With permanent theaters in five U.S. cities and Berlin, and having performed extended runs in other locations, including Canada, the UK, the Netherlands, Switzerland, and Japan, Blue Man Group has now played to more than thirty million people around the world.

For those who aren't familiar with this show, Blue Man Group offers a unique blend of performance art, music, comedy, and electronics. What universe they come from is unknown, but what the audience sees is three bald men in blue face (and blue hands) who move from one mesmerizing adventure to another, driven by a sense of innocent curiosity. They play otherworldly percussion instruments, creating stunningly colorful visuals in the process. They involve the audience in their journey of discovery in wondrous, entertaining ways.

Chris Wink is one of the original Blue Men, now serving as CEO and chief creative officer. The other two founders are Phil Stanton, who is the chief director of the stage productions, and Matt Goldman, who is the leader of the Blue School. (Yes, there is a Blue School where aspiring Blue Men go to learn their craft.)

From the beginning the three wanted Blue Man Group to grow into something bigger, but not at the expense of their creativity. They made a conscious decision to grow slowly and thoughtfully and never compromise their creative standards. This was their simplicity.

Blue Man Group had a mission: "to create amazing audience experiences." This would be the force that moved them forward and ultimately helped them grow. Throughout their existence the mission has always been the priority—not the desire to play to bigger audiences in more places.

It took a while to get things moving at all. Their first regular show, put on by outside producers, began in New York in 1991. The Blue Men literally worked for three years without a night off until their contract ran out. Only then did they become the true owners of the Blue Man show, taking control of their own destiny. That's when the slow, deliberate growth began.

Chris spoke about an amazing opportunity that opened up after Blue Man Group had become an off-Broadway phenomenon. They were offered a spot on Broadway to perform among the city's most popular shows—and turned it down.

One of the most important things we've ever done was to decline that offer. If we had gone to Broadway, we would have grown too fast—and the show would likely have closed. By staying small, we could slowly create an organization that was sort of organic. With the profit we were making, we were growing in a healthier way. We developed the ability to be a production company, which ultimately allowed us to open other venues.

The group went on to open a show in Boston in 1995. Two years later they opened a show in Chicago. Three years after that they started a show in Las Vegas. There they purposefully decided not to go the route of Cirque du Soleil, which had opened a number of shows in that entertainment paradise. To do so would have required bringing in investors, who would have exerted pressure to "really blow it out" and see how fast they could scale. Instead they opened in one venue in Las Vegas and continue in only one venue there to this day.

Growing in a controlled way meant Blue Man Group could build a lasting culture. The founders wanted new hires to feel like theirs was a "noble endeavor," going beyond mere entertainment, doing their part to ignite a bit of childlike wonder in audiences. They wanted everyone who worked in the organization—performers, musicians, production crews, and office staff—to feel like they were a part of delivering this experience.

It wasn't just fast growth that the Blue Men resisted. Chris says that in general their policy was to stay away from platforms they didn't really understand.

We didn't try to make a video game, product line, movie, television show, or cartoons. We stayed in the business we were good at. It's been more of a slow burn. We're trying to be successful, but we want to be sustainable. We want to be evergreen. Moving slow is just one of the things we've consciously chosen to do.

Chris cites Disney as an example of a business to emulate, not so much for its creative product but for its immortality. Disney knows how to keep creating new customers.

We don't just want to have a successful show. We want to have a successful company—one that thrives in the long term. So, yeah, it's fun and amazing to think of how long it's lasted, but we're still hungry to move to the next level.

This is where Chris's company faces a challenge similar to other organizations—keeping things simple as it evolves. One way Blue Man Group does that is by institutionalizing behaviors that keep the mission in focus. Because creating amazing audience experiences is what they're all about, Blue Man Group does something special prior to every performance—something the audience never even gets to see.

It's a tradition for us, and it's really kind of unheard of. On Broadway you don't have people come out and do a couple of numbers before their own show—but we always do. That's the time for the performers and crew to be free, with no audience and no ramifications. It gets them into the "head space" of Blue Man Group and establishes a collaborative vibe. It's really important to us. It's our way of talking about the mission.

Today Blue Man Group is organized like the big business it is—complete with managing director, financial office, and corporate office. But it hasn't become complex, and it hasn't lost sight of why it exists, because all three original Blue Men have done the hard work of building simplicity into their organization.

Even the simplest ideas often require many iterations to develop. Perfection takes grit, determination, and perseverance. For Blue Man Group, simplicity is the result of an extraordinary amount of work, devotion, and constant evolution. In the end, Chris believes, something wonderful happens.

> *Over time the work becomes simpler. It becomes clearer, simpler, and more elegant. The experiences we build can be complicated, but the ones that really work are the ones that are really clear. They're distilled. It takes an incredible amount of work to get something to be simple.*

To illustrate, Chris talks about how difficult it is to craft interesting transitions between scenes in any live performance when different scenes require their own stage setup. In the world of Blue Man Group, transitions have always been seen as a creative challenge. When they are cleverly executed, the audience sees them as part of the fun, though they have no idea how much effort goes into making the experience so seamless. Again, it's a lot of work behind the scenes that pays off in creating the perception of simplicity.

When Chris attends another company's production and sees a pause between scenes, it touches a nerve within.

> *I'm like, "What the heck?" I mean, it's lazy. They just stopped working too early. There's always a way to do it. You just have to work harder.*

Marketing is another part of "controlled growth" for Blue Man Group. They recognize that over more than two decades audiences have changed, and they need to keep their message relevant. There came a time when they started to feel that people who hadn't seen the show didn't really get what it was about. So they did something unexpected for a bunch of creative people—they ran focus groups with virgin audiences and the results were enlightening.

We asked what they thought the show would be like, and they really couldn't say. They said things like "They play the drums or something." They didn't have a good way of wrapping their brains around it. Or they just had a wrong impression—like "creepy mimes who have a food fight."

Afterward they took these Blue Man first-timers to see the show, then reassembled the group afterward to talk about the experience. Most of the people were surprised. The show wasn't at all what they'd expected. That made Chris and company realize that they needed to communicate the spirit of the show in a simpler way.

For Chris the effort was like psychotherapy. They started by going back to the very beginning, asking themselves, "Why did we do all of this in the first place?"

If I was to meet someone in a bar, and they asked about my life's work, what would I tell them? It certainly wasn't just about the color blue. It was something else. So what is that thing? The more we probed, the more we realized it was "a heightened experience of being alive."

That concept fit well. Onstage the performers' curious natures lead them to "discover" things in exciting and infectious ways. They bring scenes to life with unusual uses of color—more than just blue—splashing paint and using onstage electronics. Since color has always been part of Blue Man Group's DNA, they found it to be a terrific metaphor to capture the richness of the show. That led to a new campaign theme: *Dare to live in full color.*

One of the most difficult things for a company to do is to develop a theme that has authenticity. Apple's *Think different* had it, because it captured the spirit of the company going back to the days when it built its first computers in a garage. Likewise, *Dare to live in full color* describes the essence of Blue Man Group throughout its history. It invites people to toss the rules aside and better experience life. For the Blue Men a theme like this is more than marketing—it's a battle cry. It's the mission brought to life.

Chris, Phil, and Matt had a built-in advantage: They were the founders of a small company and had the power to demand simplicity as it grew larger. But the truth is, many people trying to simplify aren't in that position. Oftentimes they're part of a larger organization and must do battle with the forces of the status quo.

What then?

Creating Ownership of Simplicity

If you're not in the position to start the simplification process by decree, you'll need the support of key people in the organization. Making a company more receptive to change requires familiarity with Human Behavior 101.

Such was the case for Letha Ross-Steffey, who, as vice president of marketing planning at AMC Theatres, teamed up with the CMO and CEO to rebrand the company in 2000. (Today Letha is AMC's vice president of studio partnerships.)

Founded ninety years ago, AMC now has more than 340 movie theaters across the United States, attracting about two hundred million moviegoers annually. The rebranding succeeded in recasting AMC as a spirited company offering a quality movie experience presented in clean and comfortable multiplex theaters.

Prior to 2000, however, that image wasn't nearly as distinct. Over time the brand had grown unfocused. Customers were getting inconsistent messaging across advertising, in-theater posters and collateral, and the on-screen branding that appears before trailers and feature films. There didn't seem to be enough AMC "brand glue" to add up to a clear and simple image of the theaters in moviegoers' minds. For many customers AMC was just another movie theater. In fact, the whole trend toward giant multiplex theaters could be a turnoff to many who loved the traditional movie experience they'd grown up with.

In this atmosphere Letha set out to develop a simple and distinctive brand personality around which all the marketing efforts could be built. The goal was to build a consistently energetic and modern brand.

Letha was new at the job but thankfully had the support of CEO Gerry Lopez and CMO Stephen Colanero (who were also new to the company) in her rebranding efforts. However, whatever plan they came up with would require the support of the AMC executive team, and getting that support would be a formidable task, says Letha.

I think that this is where a lot of companies face a challenge. We believed that we needed to embark on something new. But others were holding on and embracing what had been there for a very long time.

Rather than risk alienating those whose support was necessary, she came up with a strategy to dramatically change the company's branding by making the executive team part of the adventure and bringing them along one step at a time.

First Letha commissioned a strategic partner to conduct a thorough brand study. As part of that process, the executive team was interviewed, ensuring that their opinions and perceptions became part of the study.

Letha made a point of briefing the executive team periodically as the brand study progressed, keeping them up to speed on what had been learned in a range of interviews with consumers, Wall Street analysts, studio partners, and strategic partners like Coca-Cola.

With the research completed, Letha and her group invited a number of branding and advertising agencies to pitch for AMC's business, and she again made the executive team feel like they were part of that process.

By involving the executive team in these ways, Letha and her team were able to guide AMC to the widespread and consistent branding that's visible today. The round red shape of the AMC logo is used to create "emoticons"—illustrated and animated characters that portray the positive aspects of the AMC experience, including a wide variety of films, modern comforts, and a "movie club" loyalty program.

Given the large number of AMC theaters around the country, redesigning and unifying the branding was only half the battle. Once it was approved, Letha needed to roll out the new look across all theaters. Events were held around the country to herald the arrival of the new branding and to make employees a part of the effort. Letha explains that the company reaped immediate benefits from having one consistent look and feel, internally and externally.

> *The new branding has unified everything—our website, on-screen promos, advertising, communication materials, employee name badges, HR materials, paychecks, business cards . . . every single thing.*

Because this was a radical departure from the branding that had been used for many years before, it would surely have been the source of internal trauma if the new marketing team had simply commissioned the work and tried to force it through. Rather than face a polarizing battle, Letha used a bit of human understanding to ensure that the key decision makers had a sense of ownership and participation in the redesigned AMC.

Again we see the value of involving the ultimate decision maker(s) in the process. Surprising people at the end of a process puts them in the position where they have to buy the recommendation or kill it. But when decision makers are brought into the process at key points and invited to participate, the odds of reaching a happy ending are much greater.

In effect, Letha was taking a conservative approach to reaching a bold conclusion. As an executive within an existing company with a deeply rooted culture, she had to find a creative route to a more creative place.

The task facing AMC was to solidify branding in the United States only. The task of simplifying the brand image is quite different when your issues involve multiple companies across multiple countries.

Tackling Complexity Across Borders

When Bruce Churchill became president of DirecTV Latin America, he faced a set of circumstances that were dauntingly complex. That's because

DirecTV Latin America was a single company in name only. In reality it was a collection of overlapping companies and responsibilities.

I'll spare you the head-spinning details, but the company's complexity really took root in 2003, when Rupert Murdoch's News Corp. acquired DirecTV, primarily for its U.S. operations. At that time DirecTV also had operations in Latin America, where it worked with a number of partners—some of which were in competition with other companies in the region already controlled by Murdoch.

Bruce explained that, as president of DirecTV Latin America, he was tasked with making this complicated arrangement make sense.

> *I orchestrated kind of a six-way, six-party merger. Then we, DirecTV, actually bought News Corp out of its remaining stakes in Latin America to create a single company, instead of having a separate business in each of the major territories.*

Prior to the mergers the businesses involved had about three million subscribers, with revenue of around $1 billion. Today, with a single unified brand, DirecTV Latin America has eighteen million subscribers and revenue of $8 billion to $9 billion. The only reason his business even exists today, says Bruce, is that the overall organization found a way to simplify.

The unification of these companies as a single brand was only a starting point. Before he could simplify DirecTV's operations, Bruce needed to change the reporting structure, which had evolved in complicated ways to accommodate the complex relationships.

DirecTV was organized so that the functional head of each country reported to a manager based in Florida. For example, the heads of marketing in Peru, Chile, and Colombia all reported to a single head of marketing based in Florida. The same was true of all the other business functions. This structure resulted in a huge amount of overhead sitting in Florida, overseeing business units in other countries, creating an endless flow of communication back and forth. As Bruce tells the story, this was hardly ideal.

To tell you how messed up that kind of arrangement could be, I visited Florida shortly after I started this job. Every one of these functional business heads swore to me that their part of the company was making money. But when you added it up, they were actually in bankruptcy.

It had become convoluted, and the financial reporting was designed to reflect the convoluted structure. Somehow they had all convinced themselves they were making money. Everyone was in his own little world.

Bruce's solution was to eliminate that entire organization in Florida and empower management in each country to be responsible for its own business. That meant that each country would have its own P&L, sales, marketing, HR, legal, and finance teams. Simplifying the operation into what Bruce calls "natural markets" made the new structure instantly more entrepreneurial and less behemothlike. Each country felt like it belonged to a team, instead of just being a cog in a wheel. That changed the very spirit of each operation.

Another area in need of simplification was the technology being provided to customers. When Bruce took the helm, DirecTV Latin America used a different technology platform from the one being used in the United States.

It made no sense spending money to develop a technology platform for twenty million subscribers in the U.S. and then reinvent it for Latin America. The U.S. products were better than what we had, they came out sooner, and they were well tested in the market. I could also get them cheaper, because I'd get economy of scale. It was so blindingly obvious. I can't understand how anybody thought it was a good idea to create a separate platform for Latin America.

Bruce relied upon simplicity's best friend, common sense, to embrace the U.S. technology. I was curious to get Bruce's take on what causes these "obviously wrong" decisions to rule the day.

Mostly ego, plus the related desire to control. And then sometimes people genuinely believe there are differences, having a natural bias that things need to be different in their country, when that isn't necessarily the case.

Bruce celebrates the cultural differences between the United States and Latin America. But in this case those differences were standing in the way of improving the business of all associated. The system in place simply failed the logic test.

Throughout my research for this book, leader after leader talked about making decisions that, at the end of the day, were somewhat obvious. What makes them more effective is their ability to make those decisions out of confidence, even in the face of strong opposition.

This is what puts simplicity within the grasp of every leader. It's not magic. Rather, it's the result of experience, good sense, and logic—combined with the boldness to activate it.

Simplifying Apple's Marketing Machine

Tom Suiter has an interesting history with Apple and Steve Jobs. He was hired in 1982 as Apple's internal creative director and had a personal relationship with Steve from that point on. Over the years, he was called upon by Steve to serve different functions—designer, creative director, agency chief, and creative adviser.

Tom had a front-row seat to the evolution of Steve Jobs and the ways in which he kept marketing simple as Apple grew bigger. Though Steve took some steps that made a lot of people uncomfortable—and perhaps ran afoul of some traditional rules of business—he was really just relying on instinct and common sense.

In the earliest days of Apple, Steve was trying to figure out if he should continue to use outside design agencies or if it would be better to handle design in-house. At Tom's suggestion, Steve decided on the latter, and he tasked Tom with building an internal creative services group, which ultimately numbered sixty-five people.

Generally that group did everything that the ad agency (then called Chiat\Day) did not do, including the collateral and packaging for the Apple II computer and for the Macintosh that followed. That's how it all worked until 1985, when Steve was driven from Apple following his falling out with CEO John Sculley.

Tom left Apple at the same time. His career went in a few different directions in the following years, but he kept in touch with Steve. By the time Steve bought Pixar, Tom and two colleagues had started their own design firm called CKS Partners. Steve hired CKS to work on the Pixar brand identity.

When the team was ready to present ideas for the branding that would introduce each Pixar film, John Lasseter and Steve Jobs came to the CKS office in San Francisco. A number of concepts were presented, but Tom explains that the designers had a clear favorite.

The idea was that some of the cooler characters in Pixar's movies would vie to be the i in Pixar. We cobbled together this really rough MacroMind Director animation featuring the little Luxo lamp, in which the lamp would hop out and squish the i that's there, assume its place, and stand there proudly. We showed it to Steve and John. We were all so nervous. When we finished, Steve turned to John and said, "That's not too terrible."

That's a perfectly Steve-like reaction, always leaving room for improvement. Here, though, this was exactly the branding that Pixar ended up using. It is endearingly entertaining and perfectly captures the essence of the Pixar brand.

This was all happening during the time when Steve was out of Apple and also struggling to create something new with NeXT. CKS continued to do the creative work for Pixar marketing. Then, in 1997, Steve returned to Apple and another adventure began.

At this point CKS staffed up and essentially became Apple's creative services group again, putting Tom in a role similar to the one he had played in the eighties. But Steve wasn't stopping there. He thought Apple's marketing had grown tangled and ineffective during his absence and believed that the marketing effort needed to be overhauled if Apple was to successfully reignite.

Apple's ad agency at the time was BBDO, as it had been since John Scully brought it aboard in 1985. (BBDO had been Sculley's ad agency when he was CEO of Pepsi.) At the end of Gil Amelio's time as CEO, an agency review was already taking place, says Tom.

> *Then I got that great phone call from Steve, saying, "So, I am going to fire BBDO, and I want to have some agencies pitch our business. Do you want to sit on my side of the table?"*

Tom leaped at the opportunity to see a number of agencies, all given the same briefing materials, march in and try to convince Steve they had the best strategic and creative brains. Which is exactly what happened.

Tom joined Steve as he listened to pitches from Arnold, a well-regarded creative ad agency in Boston, and what was then called TBWA\Chiat\Day. The latter was Steve's partner in crime from the early days of Apple, led by the creative legend Lee Clow. That agency had been responsible for the launch of Macintosh years earlier, making history with the "1984" ad that ran during the Super Bowl—considered by many to be the greatest commercial of all time. This ad was the first megaproduction created for the Super Bowl, starting the trend that so many companies have followed since. Ultimately Steve chose to go with Lee and company, and not long afterward the *Think different* campaign was born.

Tom had developed a deep relationship with Steve and Apple over the years and, like many, he had been saddened by the company's decline in Steve's absence. Things that had once been simple now seemed so complicated.

> *In a lot of ways Apple had become complacent in what it was doing, so scattered and unfocused. I don't recall the exact number, but Steve said*

there were like eighty-seven different initiatives going on inside Apple when he came back. He basically became very ruthless and just started killing stuff.

He wasn't killing projects for sport, although he no doubt took some pleasure in erasing certain remnants of the John Sculley years, such as the Newton, Apple's first "personal digital assistant." He was doing it to remove the distractions, just as he did by settling Apple's lawsuit against Microsoft.

Simplifying the marketing effort was also a big part of Steve's plan. Tom recalls a meeting where Steve introduced Apple's internal creative team to the CKS team. He surprised the Apple people by telling them that CKS would be doing all of the branding and design.

That was a shocker because the Apple group had considered branding and design to be their responsibility. They would now have to adjust to a new world. Upsetting as that may have been to some, Steve didn't care about politics or hurt feelings. He simply expected people to understand their responsibilities and do brilliant work.

It's not uncommon for a company to reshape its marketing department as it gets bigger, adding layers of approvals. That's what Apple had done in Steve's absence. But now that Steve was back, he quickly set out to get things back to a place where he felt more comfortable.

He made it clear that he would be directly involved with the marketing, participating as a member of the team. He didn't want to be kept in the dark as campaigns were being developed. He wanted to be part of the process.

Tom attributes Apple's success to the fact that Steve's passion for marketing was equal to his passion for technology—and he never let the company's message get complicated. His way of working was light-years away from the way Tom worked with other iconic companies, such as General Electric and United Airlines. Steve's involvement, as Tom puts it, was the ultimate simplifier.

What was really cool—and we never did this back in the Apple II days—
were our weekly meetings. I mean, how often do people get the chance
to work directly with the CEO of a company, put work in front of him,
and have him simply say, "Give me that—that's what I want"? There was
no endless debate and no asking for a dozen other opinions. It was just
"Do that."

Even when there was no new work to discuss, Steve insisted on having
the regular meetings. He would use them as opportunities to talk about
whatever was on his mind. It gave everyone on the team a feeling of involvement and responsibility.

Following Apple's near-bankruptcy in 1997, a national magazine ran
a story about Apple's newfound success. The article included a photo-
graph of Steve sitting at a table with Avie Tevanian (software), Phil Schiller
(product marketing), and several others. On the table were some iBook
advertising materials, as well as some product packaging. To Tom that
photo says it all.

That was how we did stuff! That way everyone knew what everyone else
was working on. Steve just had the intuition to say, "We should really do
this every week."

Steve didn't do these things because he'd had a formal business education. He hadn't. He just had an instinct for running a big company like it
was a small company, with a sharp focus and minimal layers. He put the
most talented people in the right places, simplified areas of responsibility,
and attended regular meetings so that he—as the ultimate decision
maker—would be actively involved.

Many leaders can relate to the dilemma Steve faced when he returned
to the company in 1997. The ability to move a company forward is often
constrained by layers of complexity that have built up over many years—
mostly in the name of efficiency.

In such cases simplification is certainly a challenge. But as Steve proved, it is never out of reach.

Taming the Beast Within

On the day I was to meet with Robert Nason, a member of the leadership team at Australia's biggest telecom company, Telstra, I had lunch with a friend in Sydney. When I told her about the book I was writing and how thrilled I was that Robert had agreed to be interviewed for it, she winced.

"If you want your book to have any credibility, do *not* use Telstra as an example," she said. She went on to tell me multiple tales of woe, all involving the monolithic Telstra and its monolithically bad customer service. In her opinion, Telstra was the poster child for complexity. To properly do battle, she had actually kept a log of the many conversations she'd had with customer service without ever solving her issues. Her log went on for pages.

As I would soon discover, my friend's story would actually resonate well with Robert. The abundance of frustrating customer experiences with Telstra was one big reason he had been brought into the company in 2010 as group executive of business support and improvement. He made no bones about the fact that there was still a lot to be done on Telstra's journey to simplicity.

What Robert saw in Telstra was a company that had come down with a bad case of big-company syndrome. Processes and procedures had grown quite complex, causing frustration for employees and customers alike.

Robert says that Telstra's troubles were so well known that when he joined the company on a mission to fix things, one news organization reported his appointment by saying he'd just taken "the worst job in corporate Australia."

We were the market's worst performer in customer service. After three profit warnings, our CEO said that one more would cost him his job. To

win our customers back, we had to dig out of that hole. We had to ask,
"What do our customers want?" And simplicity was a key understanding.

While many describe Robert as a cost cutter, he considers himself a simplifier. He's out to reduce processes and eliminate burdensome bureaucracy—which does reduce costs but also creates a far simpler organization. When he started, Robert estimated the simplification process would result in about $2 billion in cuts. Three years into the process, he believes the cuts were more like $9 billion or $10 billion.

Robert flatly states that simplification itself isn't the goal. Rather, it's a means to achieve the goal, which is more satisfied customers and a more inspiring workplace. In Robert's thinking, simplicity is "the fundamental fabric of delivering."

We're big on creating customers who love you and want to tell their
friends and family about you. You don't do that by impressing customers
with how complex everything is. It's the opposite. You make things very
simple for them.

Similar to Brian Hartzer's view is Robert's belief that there is a mechanism at work in big companies that creates complexity. Smart, well-meaning people are often driven to demonstrate their talent, experience, or ability to manage. In many cases, creating new processes is more about protecting one's job than making things simpler.

You really have to work hard to unwind that kind of thinking. You can
be smart by coming across very, very simply in what you do. That's one of
the things we've had to work on as a leadership team.

Typically, says Robert, when people in big companies perceive that a process is important to success, they follow that process blindly. For example, when Telstra employees were called upon to give a presentation, they would dutifully prepare a deck that typically contained one slide for every thirty seconds of the presentation—regardless of what might best serve the topic.

He noticed another big-company behavior in people's unwillingness to suggest deep change, mostly for fear of jeopardizing their jobs. Rather than dig into issues at their most basic level to find a better solution, people would simply edit, adding something new on top of what was already there. Either that or they would come up with a work-around, getting around the problem without really fixing it.

"Work-around," of course, is just another term for complexity. And complexity has a way of breeding more complexity.

Robert's team found that parts of Telstra's basic structure were actually promoting complexity. One good example was a group known as Error Provisioning. Because they were the ones who received customer problems, this group had developed an inflated sense of importance. It was almost as if they didn't want the company to be perfect, because they existed to correct things. It was, Robert says, a self-fulfilling prophecy at work.

Telstra was measuring its ability to solve problems using the numbers reported by Error Provisioning. On average it took five days to resolve a problem. A complicated organization might aim to reduce that number by some acceptable percentage. In Robert's thinking, incremental change at Telstra would have little impact. It wouldn't change public opinion of the company and it wouldn't inspire employees. And a company that talks about how much error it is willing to accept is only promoting incremental change. That's a lesson he took from Apple.

Steve Jobs had a vision of the way things should be. He wasn't interested in baby steps and incremental change. It's the final goal that sets expectations and motivates people to achieve.

Robert decided that the goal should not be to reduce errors by some percentage. The goal should be that nothing goes to Error Provisioning at all. Clearly communicating that target to employees in unmistakable terms gave Telstra a better chance of improving with bigger, more noticeable results.

When Robert first arrived at Telstra, he saw that the company didn't have a culture of customer service or innovation. In fact, there wasn't much of a culture at all. The company was set up in silos, so people didn't have the opportunity to exchange views or get to know one another better. It had been years since they'd last held an off-site meeting to talk about mission and values.

Robert's first order of business was to involve the workforce in the discussion, to encourage them to join the effort to fix what was broken, and to make sure they understood that Telstra was deeply committed to change.

We wanted people to think, "This mob is serious about it and is going about it right away."

Robert brought together over seven thousand team leaders in the company in groups of seventy or eighty. Five of Telstra's top two hundred executives attended every session, as did one of the senior executives reporting directly to the CEO.

The main purpose was to say that we want to get this fixed, and we need to go through this together if we're going to get it right.

Everyone seemed to have a "my Telstra story." They talked about why they had come to the company and the good things they believed the company was capable of achieving. Many of their stories were emotional, given that some families had worked with the company for generations.

One thing that came up often was the concept of the "barbecue conversation," which is a very Australian thing. Many said that when they were at a barbecue and it came out that they worked for Telstra, people seemed compelled to tell their individual horror stories about their experience with the company. From the CEO down, Telstra employees seemed unable to escape these conversations. And the stories they heard were harrowing.

People want to be proud of their company and not have to rise to its defense in their off-hours. So, upon hearing that management was serious about improving, employees were eager to help.

Robert asked employees to think of ways Telstra could simplify the customer experience. He brought the top two hundred Telstra people together twice each year to discuss how the changes were working and how they could be made to work better.

The initial meetings focused on the experiences of those who had front-line contact with customers—retail employees, installers, and technicians. These were the people who were taking the heat from customers when things didn't work right. These meetings were a pivotal experience for Robert.

We spent the first meeting listening to calls coming into the contact center, when customers were complaining about their experience. Our support people explained what it's like to be on the front line and what Telstra's performance was doing to them. It got very personal. I had a vision of this company, and this wasn't it. We had to get things fixed down in the field.

To further demonstrate Telstra's commitment internally, it was decided that the entire executive team would become more visible to employees. The executives had a short training session, then jumped on the phone lines themselves to deal with customers' problems. These calls were filmed and shared throughout the company.

It showed that we were in there, that we want to understand, that we want to get a taste of what the front line is going through.

This experience led to the creation of a new initiative within the company that grew to include more than 7,500 people. Those who worked directly with customers were given a stronger voice in the company. Those who worked in a retail shop or doing in-home repairs could now feed what they observed and experienced directly to management so the company could take action to fix processes that needed fixing.

Like any public company, Telstra must be transparent about how it's doing. It's required to submit guidance to the market as to how it expects to perform in the coming quarter. Three times in Robert's first year Telstra told the market, "We had it wrong, and we're not going to make as much profit as we want." Three months later it was "Sorry, it's actually worse than we thought, and profit will be going down again." The same sad message was delivered yet a third time.

As a result, Telstra's share price dropped nearly 30 percent. However, the changes enacted by Robert's team have had a visible effect. In the first three years of the company's drive to simplify, the share price more than doubled. Market share increased in every category.

I think that now everyone would say that even when we don't get it right, we care. That alone is a big change from where we were.

Any big company contemplating an effort to simplify would be wise to understand how and why Telstra was able to make the strides it did. Though Robert had a very big boulder to push uphill, he also had a clear role, a blank slate, and a charter from the Telstra board to go anywhere within the company and take whatever actions were necessary.

In his first twelve months he was able to initiate over thirty simplification projects. He questioned processes, redesigned structures, and eliminated inefficiencies. The turning point, says Robert, was getting momentum on his side.

It's much easier now, because the team believes. It's so much easier to keep momentum going when you take the complexities away and employees like what they're doing. People like to simplify things. They take pride in it. They want to show me how they've done that.

Again we see that employees in big companies are typically eager to change and quick to embrace the idea of simplification. It's complexity that sends people running in the opposite direction.

Robert is proof that the CEO himself doesn't have to take personal command of simplifying a big company. The effort can be just as successful if the authority is given to someone else. What's essential is for simplicity to have a champion, and that champion must be empowered.

The changes at Telstra are ongoing. Robert was clear with me that after three years the company was only about halfway to its target state. To him, that would be a place where employees feel motivated and empowered by a simple mission, which would in turn boost customer satisfaction and create positive word of mouth.

Asked what has been his most important accomplishment to date, Robert didn't hesitate for a second. He said it was winning the hearts and minds of the workforce. That's the first step in building a simpler company and it leads directly to a better customer experience.

When the Going Gets Tough, the Tough Get Simpler

There is a perception that when it comes to simplicity, big companies exist in various states of hopelessness. One of the most gratifying parts of my research was finding companies that have so convincingly proven otherwise.

When organizations the size of Hyundai Card, Westpac Bank, and Telstra can make visible strides in simplicity, there's no excuse for any big company not trying. Even more important, there's no excuse for not succeeding. No matter how complex a business might be, the desire to simplify is alive inside the psyche of the workforce, and it's within the power of any business leader to activate it.

In fact, the more complicated a workplace is, the more eager people will be to participate in creating change. Simplicity wins friends quickly.

It's hard to imagine the enormity of the task that confronted Robert Nason at Telstra as he attempted to make a giant telecom simpler and more responsive to its customers. But as we saw in Telstra's turnaround, amazing things can be accomplished when a company moves forward one step at a time.

As Brian Hartzer demonstrated at Westpac Bank, simplification can sometimes be accomplished by swimming upstream—finding the simpler version of a product, service, or process that has suffered too many "improvements" over time, ultimately becoming unwieldy or burdensome.

It's safe to say that every successful operation—no matter how big— was less complicated in its past. It's likely that the simpler version of your company still exists, though it may be hidden beneath the complexities that have multiplied over time.

Of course, even better than finding a way to remove complexity is charting a course to insulate the company against becoming complicated, as Blue Man Group did more than twenty years ago.

If your company is suffering the effects of complexity, take heart in the fact that this is not a terminal condition. It is indeed reversible. You may be surprised how quickly the seeds of simplicity take root.

Chapter 7
Simplicity Is Sleeker

At an early age we learn that the laws of physics can help us improve the ways we move a physical object from one place to another.

We can move a stationary object more easily if we lessen its weight. We can reduce drag by making an object more aerodynamic. We can use less force by pushing an object along a smooth surface instead of a textured one. And so on.

Conceptually, simplicity is the means by which we can achieve a similar effect in the world of business. We can help move a company faster by removing friction, making processes more aerodynamic, and helping customers see more clearly.

In short, simplicity has the power to change the physics of business, removing the obstacles that get in the way of employees and customers alike.

The Skunkworks Principle

In your professional life you may have heard people talking about creating a "skunkworks" group to handle a special project.

The term has a colorful history. In 1943, Lockheed Aircraft Corporation (now Lockheed Martin) was approached by the military to quickly create a new aircraft in response to the escalating German threat. The key word being "quickly." To do this, they created a special unit called Skunk Works, a reference to the moonshine factory in the old comic strip *L'il Abner*.

Skunk Works comprised a team of engineers that could move faster, operating outside the normal corporate confines. In fact, it actually operated out of a rented circus tent. The project was a success, the new plane was designed ahead of schedule, and Skunk Works continues to be a part of Lockheed to this day.

The key engineer on the team was a man named Kelly Johnson, who lived by the motto "Be quick, be quiet, be on time," which is certainly good advice for any business. Even more appropriate for this book, his favorite maxim was "Keep it simple, stupid." Very impressive for a man who engineered such complex technology.

Kelly was so good at his job, he was offered the presidency of Lockheed on three occasions. However, he declined each time because he preferred to oversee the Skunk Works. He liked the agility and freedom he enjoyed as part of that group.

Kelly's success is described on Lockheed Martin's website today:

> *What allowed Kelly to operate the Skunk Works so effectively and efficiently was his unconventional organizational approach. He broke the rules, challenging the current bureaucratic system that stifled innovation and hindered progress.**

In other words, he would have fit well in any company wishing to streamline its operations today.

When I hear about skunkworks operations achieving success within bigger organizations, I'm reminded of something I once heard at an open-mike night in a San Francisco comedy club. An aspiring comic marveled

---

* http://www.lockheedmartin.com/us/aeronautics/skunkworks/origin.html.

at the black boxes in airplanes for their seeming indestructibility. Planes can crash, burn, freeze, or sit at the bottom of the ocean for months, but somehow the black boxes always survive. He wondered, "Why don't they just make the whole plane out of that stuff?"

One could make a similar observation about the skunkworks concept in business today. If a company can achieve simpler, faster, better results with a skunkworks group, why not make the whole company out of that stuff?

Obviously, I oversimplify. A global powerhouse can't be run by a bunch of guys in a circus tent. (Although some may appear to be.) But the principle at the core of the skunkworks concept can be a source of inspiration when you embark upon a program of simplification.

I invite you to consider how you might set up your company if you were starting from scratch today—without the bureaucracy and without the constraints of processes that have accumulated over the years. The essence of the skunkworks concept is really "stepping outside the system" to create something that works faster and better, freeing people to do their best work in a more frictionless environment.

Earlier in this book we heard from Joe Mimran, who created the Joe Fresh fashion brand in Canada under the auspices of the giant Loblaws supermarket chain. According to Joe, one of the reasons Joe Fresh was so successful was that he started this business in a skunkworks format.

> *We were almost like an outsourced component. This is what allowed us to do what we did within this behemoth company. We were physically detached, in different locations. We couldn't operate the way the parent company did. That was the only way I could attract top creative talent.*

Joe, like Kelly Johnson at Lockheed, set up an operation that was physically apart from the larger company. But the idea of skunkworks transcends real estate. It's also a frame of mind, an openness to new ideas that can lead to a more streamlined operation.

One good way to start thinking the skunkworks way is to step back and see your own products and services as your customers do. What you observe may not be as simple as you think.

Optimizing Choice

Many companies have a view of choice that isn't really supported by the facts. Flawed logic leads them to believe that if they give customers more choices, they'll get better results.

In his book *The Paradox of Choice*, Barry Schwartz says exactly the opposite. He explains how today's explosion of choices creates anxiety in customers and often induces decision-making paralysis. Proponents of simplicity no doubt agree.

Neil Hunt, chief product officer of Netflix, as a member of that group. He cites Schwartz's thesis in describing the results of a Netflix experiment. The company tried adding a half-star option to the five-star rating system people use to rate films. The thinking was that a more accurate rating system would be more appealing to viewers. But when Netflix implemented the half-star format, the use of viewer ratings dropped by 11 percent. Too much choice had a negative effect.

John McGrath cites the paradox of choice in the real estate industry as well. The more choices you provide to a client, says John, the more difficult their decision becomes. He's not a fan of the "kitchen sink" approach of throwing a lot of things at people until they finally make a choice, even though many realtors do exactly that.

In general, what people prefer is the right choice—not endless choice. Yet endless choice is what so many companies seem to strive for. That desire makes them particularly susceptible to the virus called product proliferation. This is more likely to clog the selling process than enhance it.

In the computer world one doesn't have to look too far to find examples of choices run amok. At the end of 2015, HP offered fifty-seven choices in desktop computers and sixty-one in laptops. Over at Dell I found thirty models of desktops and twenty-three laptops.

Poor Apple. You can count its different computer models on about five fingers. But then, we all know that Apple isn't poor at all. Though it offers dramatically fewer computer models than its competitors, Apple's share of profits in the PC industry is currently more than HP's and Dell's combined, and has been for several years running.

What Apple offers its customers isn't so much a lack of choice—it's a lack of confusion. That's a very attractive proposition. As was true when Steve Jobs slashed the product offerings back in 1998, offering fewer choices allows Apple to focus its resources on quality and design, which in turn reinforces the Apple brand and allows the company to price its products at a premium.

A more down-to-earth example can be found in the fast-food industry. Those who live in California and five other western U.S. states are familiar with a chain called In-N-Out Burger. Two things are striking about this operation: The locations are almost always packed, and the menu board is incredibly simple. In fact, at In-N-Out you can order only six things. Basically, it's a burger or a burger with a side of fries.

Compare that with McDonald's, which only at the end of 2015 started to climb out of a prolonged financial slump. From 2004 to 2014 its menu had grown by 75 percent, presenting customers with more than a hundred different dining options. According to global restaurant consultant Aaron Allen, McDonald's has created "a menu so complex, it confuses guests and takes twice as long as industry standards to prepare."*

In-N-Out subscribes to the "do fewer things better" philosophy, which has helped the company build a cult of customers. The menu contributes the "fewer" part, while quality, freshness, and service combine to create the "better."

Doing fewer things better can have an almost magical effect, creating a deeper connection with customers. What it says, and says so well, is that a company truly understands its customers. In the case of In-N-Out, it's resulted in extraordinary loyalty. The chain sells branded merchandise in most locations and people actually buy it. Try that, McDonald's.

---

* https://www.linkedin.com/pulse/10-mcstakes-mcdonalds-made-aaron-d-allen.

Choice is a strategy, and it has an impact on the way people perceive your company—as do the names you put on those choices.

Simplicity, Thy Name Is . . .

Every manufacturer knows how difficult it is to arrive at the perfect product name. Even if you succeed in developing one, it can be frustratingly difficult to get legal clearance for it.

How difficult it is for you, of course, is of little concern to customers. People simply react to what's before them. Product names send a clear message about a company's personality and its ability to simplify buying decisions. The biggest barrier to creating a sensible and appealing naming structure is product proliferation. Having too many products makes it easy for a company to get lost in a sea of meaningless words, letters, and numbers.

Once again, the computer industry provides a vivid demonstration. Look at HP's laptop offerings (strewn across many different pages on its site) and you'll be confronted with a dizzying array of product names that don't follow any discernible logic—including Z240, ProDesk, EliteDesk, Z1, Z230, Z840, ENVY, ENVY Phoenix, ENVY 750qe, Pavilion, and Sprout by HP. Dell suffers a similar condition.

Let's not leave ASUS out of this. It's divided its laptop offerings into different series, including ZenBook Series, N Series, E Series, K/A Series, and so on. And if you had your heart set on the E Series, which model would you prefer—the E402MA or the EeeBook X205TA? Your synapses will sputter as you try to decipher these product names.

Over at Apple things are far less complicated. Every laptop is simply a variation of a Mac. There's the MacBook Air, MacBook, and MacBook Pro. It's hard to imagine a naming scheme any simpler. Apple products are easy to shop for and easy to reference in conversation. Every name reflects the brand or subbrand, and this simplicity isn't lost on customers.

One of the unfair advantages Apple has when it comes to naming is that it doesn't sell many products at all. Remember, Steve Jobs pointed out that the company's entire product line could fit on a single table. Other computer makers are perfectly free to simplify their product offerings as well. They just don't.

Of course, the nature of some companies—like brick-and-mortar retailers—is such that they need to carry tens of thousands of products. Even then, simplicity stands ready to do its job.

Making Many Choices Feel Simpler

In discussing Apple's purposefully small selection of laptop models, I left out one little detail: Once you select an Apple laptop, you can configure it more than forty different ways. There is complexity there, but what Apple has done so well is to create the perception of simplicity.

This perception is something any company can achieve, no matter how complex its line of products or services. In the world of retail one company that has done this remarkably well is The Container Store. CEO Kip Tindell talks about his company's challenge:

> We have the best selection of hangers in the world. We have the best selection of trash cans in the world. We have the best selection of hooks. While others have four solutions, we have a hundred and four. But I am also very aware that too much selection can freeze people into inaction.

Understanding that too much choice can be confusing but that extensive choice is one of the top attractions at his stores, Kip found a way to offer all those products while also nurturing the perception of simplicity. He does it with terrific service, which comes in the form of "high-hospitality employees." It's the employees' job to know the customers and the products so they can quickly guide people to the product that's perfect for them.

> I think I'm familiar with Monet. But if I have a guide with me in the museum, or even just the audio-tour earphones, my appreciation level is

so much higher. Likewise, I'm more likely to find the right trash can as a result of having that guide—the salesperson who takes the time to understand and help me.

Kip has cultivated a combination of quality selection and quality attention—a wide range of solutions with expert assistance. It's that total experience that makes a customer more likely to return, he says.

They love the product so much, it just makes them smile. That's right— even a trash can make a customer smile. It just fits perfectly in that corner; it's exactly right; the customer didn't expect to find one that was so right.

Maybe it's because our lives tend to involve compromise that it feels so good when we buy something that feels exactly right. In Kip lingo this is called "getting the customer to dance." As he tells the tale, a woman might so love the closet that The Container Store built for her that she does a bit of a dance every time she looks at it. (If not a physical dance, then maybe a mental one.) This is the key to building the store's business—because that customer will want to show off the closet to her neighbor, which may inspire that neighbor to get the same thing, and then *she'll* do the dance.

Apple, in effect, curates a small number of premium products and invites premium customers to buy into its ecosystem. The Container Store operates in a different universe, says Kip, offering thousands of products from a legion of manufacturers.

I think it's wrong to believe you are such a good curator or editor that you know what everyone wants. You don't. People are too different. So you want to give them the best selection—but you also want to give them the best knowledge and service to go with it. That's when you get the greatest emotion out of your customers.

The challenge for many retailers is to discover alluring products, make deals with manufacturers, and get products into the stores as quickly as possible. Clothing stores like Topshop, H&M, and Uniqlo have to move like quicksilver to stay on top of the fashions of each season.

This is not how The Container Store succeeds. It has a niche to itself, so it can take longer to choose its products and get them into the store. It has long-term relationships with vendors and a long-term, enduring collection of merchandise.

> *Stores like Uniqlo change out their whole universe maybe every three months. Today we still sell many of the same products we opened the store with in 1978.*

Inventory at The Container Store does change, but it does so in a different, controllable way. The company regularly culls the bottom 5 percent or 10 percent of products to bring in new ones. "Like Jack Welch did with people," says Kip. But what The Container Store purposefully does not do is change out large portions of the store for any season.

> *What's important for us is the quality of the product. We hope it will be enduring. The next item we come up with and add to the store, well . . . I hope it's there for the next fifty years.*

For shoppers at The Container Store, the key to simplicity is the attention they get from the sales staff. That's what removes the friction from the shopping experience when dealing with such a vast inventory. With a helping hand from an expert who cares, they can walk into the store with a need and walk out with the right solution. This sets The Container Store apart from such competitors as Bed Bath & Beyond, where the love of customers is less visible.

Down in Australia, Westpac Bank also found a way to connect a variety of customers to a variety of products and make it all feel very simple.

The Magic Matrix of Simplicity

A single act of simplification can have a large impact in any business, but particularly so in the world of banking, where complexity has been known to hold the upper hand.

When Brian Hartzer took the job of CEO at Westpac Bank, he observed that the bank excelled at providing product choices but that in some cases too many choices were having a negative effect. He was reminded of Apple's solution to that problem.

> *I once heard a story about Steve Jobs—how in an early board meeting upon his return to the company, he had all the different Apple products up on a shelf. One by one, he started taking them off the shelf and putting them on the floor. Finally only a few were left, and he said, "Now this is what we're going to do."*

In a sense this is how Brian went about changing Westpac. At that time Westpac offered a bewildering assortment of credit card products. That didn't make a lot of sense, because there are basically just a few general categories of credit cards a customer might want—low-interest cards, cash-back cards, frequent flyer cards, etc. Further, the bank serves a finite range of customer segments, including young people just starting out, working adults, retirees, and wealthy people with complex needs.

> *If you think about customer needs along these lines, you can create a matrix. What I essentially said to my people is that within each cell of that matrix, you can have one product. That's it.*

The result was a vastly simpler, single-page matrix of products. Every credit card that did not fit in the matrix would be removed. Streamlining the product choices in this way made it easier for the frontline salespeople to explain the options to customers and easier for customers to make a selection. Brian says this decision produced real results.

Since we simplified our choices, growth of credit cards has increased dra-matically. I wouldn't say it is all because of the simplification, but that certainly has been a contributing factor. Our frontline people are no longer confused by our offerings, and that gives them more confidence when they talk to customers. It's easier to answer people's questions.

This same type of product culling took place at Hyundai Card in Seoul in an effort to make choices simpler for customers. From thirty-two credit cards being offered in 2004—all in line with competitors' offerings—Ted Chung condensed the line to only four distinct cards, with some variations in fees allowing for those wishing to add services. This was another big factor in that company's revitalization. Removing complexity made it far easier for people to choose the right card—and to value their relationship with Hyundai Card as a result.

Brian Hartzer saw another opportunity to simplify, this time in West-pac's fee structure, which wasn't exactly building customer love at the time. There were different plans with different fees charged for varying numbers of transactions beyond the first ten. This provided options for some, but it was adding complexity for others (including the salespeople).

To simplify, Westpac introduced a product with a flat fee of five dollars per month and called it the "all you need" account. Once again complexity went down and sales went up. In fact, this type of account became the leading product sold across all Westpac offices nationwide. Per Brian:

I think the theme of simplicity leading to confidence in the sales staff is very important. It may be underappreciated. Also, simplifying the prod-ucts has a ripple effect when you start getting into processes and control processes and downstream technology costs.

The changes Brian brought to Westpac clearly demonstrated the busi-ness value of streamlining. By distilling product lines and removing com-plexity from products, Westpac has made its products easier to use and easier to explain, with benefits for all associated.

Now, just as products and services can become more complicated over time, so can the processes that define a company's workings. One could say that "process proliferation" is a leading cause of complexity in business today.

Leaders with a passion for simplicity are able to see processes as one more thing in need of streamlining.

Judgment Is the Best Process

At SEEK in Australia, CEO Andrew Bassat shared his point of view about the nature of processes at different stages of a company's growth, and the shackling effect that too much process can produce.

When you're ten people, he says, processes are not really an issue. Communication just happens, because everyone knows what everyone else is doing. It's when your company grows to more than a hundred people that complex processes begin to take root. That's in response to things starting to slip between the cracks, or people getting hired who probably shouldn't have been hired. You must come to grips with the fact that you've gotten bigger. You can no longer assume business will happen the right way just because that's how it's always happened before.

> *So we do need a bit of process. Otherwise we're at risk of having too little focus and too much chaos, rather than at risk of being overbureaucratic. The process we require is to make sure everyone is fully informed, communications are on, and we have some consistency.*

Though he understands the need for process, Andrew looks at heavy process with disdain. He rejects processes that require people to conform to a rigid template, or base decisions on testing, or generally feel like managers are looking over their shoulder. He trusts in his people and in his culture to guide them.

> *If you're ruled by processes, you don't need judgment—and I prefer judgment to process.*

A terrific example of judgment triumphing over process can be found at Netflix, where cofounder Reed Hastings instituted an "unlimited vacation" policy for all employees. In an interview with *Bloomberg Businessweek* Hastings said that the policy "requires mature, responsible employees who care about high-quality work." This eliminates paperwork and allows Netflix to judge people on what they get done, rather than how many days they work. Other companies are starting to offer unlimited vacation or flexible time-off policies as well. It discourages process and encourages judgment.

Over at The Container Store, CEO Kip Tindell also talked about preferring judgment over process. He believes that if people share the company's values, they'll act in the company's best interest without being burdened by formal processes. That's why he believes so passionately in reinforcing the The Container Store's Foundation Principles, which, as we heard earlier, describe the values that are at the heart of the company's culture. These principles are kept alive by good communication, good managers, and a minimum of hierarchy, rendering intricate processes unnecessary. As Kip puts it, "We swat down processes."

StubHub cofounder Jeff Fluhr is another who takes a stand against excessive processes. Recognizing that a company needs some light structure as it grows, he believes in "process with purpose." If there isn't a clear and distinct reason to adopt a process, it will likely distract from the company's real work.

> *Process should not stifle creativity. It can't end up being a barrier to innovation or to the fluid movement of ideas. There has to be balance. And that's probably more judgment than some sort of special formula.*

When you streamline processes, you're putting more faith in people. You're building a culture of values instead of a cold framework of rules and procedures. As important, you're removing the quicksand that so often holds companies back.

Less Process Equals More Speed

In an earlier chapter we saw how Ted Chung, an unconventional leader in South Korea, was able to restore Hyundai Card to profitability when it was deeply in the red.

Because the company competes in a fast-moving industry, one of Ted's highest priorities was giving the company faster reflexes, which he did by streamlining the decision-making process. He explains:

> *A decision might take more than a month at some companies. It takes only one day here. This is the greatest weapon we have.*
>
> *I often say that we are not competing with stupid people. Over time our competitors inevitably become a lot smarter. It is unreasonable to expect that they will make mistakes. The only way we can win the battle is to not only make good decisions but to move twice as fast as they do.*

For decisions big and small Ted shuns the idea of a formal process to consider options, because that just takes more time. Instead he'll often hold a real-time discussion online or have a quick exchange via email.

As an example, Ted tells the story of an opportunity that came the company's way in 2012. Hyundai Card sometimes sponsors major concerts for its customers, and Lady Gaga had expressed a willingness to visit South Korea. The sponsorship for this event, Ted learned, would require an investment of more than a million dollars.

> *In other companies it's "I'll talk to my boss," and then "My boss will talk to his boss," and so on. That kind of thing might drag on for weeks or months. To us it's either yes or no. We are very crisp. We're fast and simple. We came to a decision in two hours.*

That decision brought Lady Gaga to Seoul and contributed enormously to the enhancement of the brand. In 2015 Hyundai Card continued its commitment to great entertainment by sponsoring Paul McCartney's first concert in South Korea—a decision that was equally swift.

This is the kind of agility you'd expect to find in a start-up, yet Ted has managed to build it into his big company's culture. He's fine with basic processes but won't tolerate layers of process that slow things down. To the contrary, he celebrates ideas that speed things up.

Another way to reduce friction in favor of speed is to make sure debate doesn't drag on. Ted enforces a strict "disagree and commit" policy. Debate is encouraged, but all must embrace the final decision. Ted doesn't tolerate those who sit quietly in a meeting and then speak negatively about the decision afterward.

Earlier we heard from Ron Johnson, who spoke about the problems he encountered at JCPenney in his attempts to simplify that organization. His quest was made more difficult for this very reason—people appearing to agree with the way forward but having different opinions upon leaving the room. It's a thorny area where "nice" leaders can hurt their own chances of success by not being tough enough.

Speed, of course, is a critical factor for any company. This is especially true for Quantcast, whose business is conducted in microseconds. Quantcast connects advertisers to relevant Internet audiences around the world in real time, based on its highly sophisticated technology.

Founder and CEO Konrad Feldman emphasizes the importance of not allowing people to get bogged down in process. It's his company's culture of openness and rapid development that has kept things simple. The culture is so strong, Konrad doesn't need to take extraordinary measures to fend off complexity.

Though Konrad's competitors may have an advantage in terms of size and resources, Quantcast has the advantage of being nimble. It has the ability to iterate, explore, and respond more quickly, which is a direct result of the company's lack of heavy process. Says Konrad:

> *One should be acutely aware of the need to be nimble and to foster a culture where people feel they can get things done. When people start to*

feel resistance, they stop trying. And if you get to that point, your pace of
innovation will grind to a halt—and you're done.

Now that we've heard a number of leaders talk about the danger of
process overload, here's an interesting twist to the tale. As it turns out, one
of the most effective tools for simplification can be—stay with me—a
process.

Distilling Simplicity from Complexity

Laura Anderson is an American businesswoman transplanted to Australia
who specializes in business strategy.

One could say she has a few things on her plate. Laura is chairman of
her own company, Strategic Vision Global; chairman of the Virgin Australia Melbourne Fashion Festival, which drew over 380,000 attendees in 2015;
and director and board member of the Australian Grand Prix Corporation.
She was previously national partner in charge of strategy and development
for the global consulting firm KPMG for more than a decade.

Laura believes simplicity is the key to arriving at a brilliant strategy.
Somewhat ironically, her means to getting there is to first immerse herself
in complexity and then take her clients through a process. She invites them
to download every bit of information they have, which can be a boatload.
Laura explains:

> *I want to see it all, because I know that the essence is in there. It's from*
> *all that information that you'll see the light and find the right path*
> *forward.*

To distill this information to its essence, Laura uses what she believes
is the most powerful tool in the pursuit of simplicity. She calls it the Rule
of Three. She asks a company to take a long, hard look at itself and decide
what three things it needs most to gain a competitive advantage. It's all
about achieving focus.

If you apply these three things relentlessly, everything gets simpler. It brings clarity to a discussion, and a purpose.

Laura has successfully used the Rule of Three to develop strategies in defense, in fashion, in the Grand Prix, and in the running of her day-to-day life.

But developing a strategy is only part of Laura's task. "Operationalizing" it is the real goal. That is, activating the strategy throughout the company and raising the organization's levels of efficiency and effectiveness. So the Rule of Three helps her arrive at the strategy, and that in turn becomes part of her "Strategy on a Page." This is exactly what it sounds like—a single sheet of paper, formatted and designed for clarity, that becomes the blueprint for putting a strategy to work.

My eyes lit up when Laura stressed the importance of the single page, because the concept is uncannily similar to something I know well from my advertising life—the creative brief. This is the document given to the creative team charged with creating an ad campaign. There's nothing worse or more confusing than being handed a creative brief that's several pages long, crammed with every possible fact an account manager or strategist could gather. Breakthrough work rarely results from such complexity.

In fact, some of the best creative people in the advertising industry refuse to even think about starting work until they're given a brief that fits on a single page. And no cheating with small font sizes and reduced margins allowed. Creating a one-page brief is an exercise that forces people to condense and simplify their thinking.

Laura's Strategy on a Page helps a company figure out where it is today, as well as what trends have led it to this point. With that information the company's leaders can drill down to where they want to be, by when, and how they will get there. This includes clarifying vision, mission, values, goals, and other factors critical to achieving success. Laura explains:

We are relentless in our pursuit. We don't have long, drawn-out strategy sessions. We have short, sharp meetings. We ask simple questions. But again, we want everything on the table. Because if you dismiss complexity, you'll never get to its essence. You have to get it all, and then you can distill it.

It's important to note the philosophical differences between Laura's approach and that of leaders who are well experienced in the art of simplification. The latter might become quite cranky churning through all that complexity to build their Strategy on a Page, preferring to rely more on instinct. But many companies are in such an advanced state of complexity that they can benefit by taking the time to go through a smart and sensible simplification process.

Both approaches can be successful. In either case what's required is belief in the power of simplicity and commitment to achieving it.

Preserving the Small-Company Spirit

In an earlier chapter I shared the story of Kofola, a favorite soft drink from Czechoslovakia's past that was revived by entrepreneur Kostas Samaras after the Velvet Revolution gave birth to the Czech Republic.

After Jannis Samaras succeeded his father as CEO of the Kofola Group, the company continued to grow. Like all companies on an upward trajectory, it had to evolve to keep pace with its success.

To satisfy demand Kofola expanded its workforce. To keep up with modern consumer tastes it added fruit juices and water to its product line. All of this made for a vibrant business, but as the company got bigger, Jannis became concerned with the side effects of success. He felt that Kofola was running afoul of one of the more important Rules of Simple: It was behaving more like a big company and less like the upstart that had recaptured the hearts of the people.

Hearing Jannis tell this story reminded me of various ad agency meetings I've attended with company leaders who were intolerant of complexity. If they perceived that our process was becoming too formal or overanalytical, they might well respond by giving us a virtual slap in the face: "You're acting like a big agency!" That was their warning that we were sacrificing creativity for efficiency, which is something they would never accept.

Jannis came to realize what had happened. To oversee the growth, Kofola had hired people with experience in big, international companies. Some of those people brought with them behaviors associated with the big companies from whence they came. They focused less on keeping the brand simple and more on systems, structures, reports, and administrative processes. And this didn't sit well with Jannis.

After four years I realized that this wasn't the company I wanted to work in. Our spirit had changed. The atmosphere was colder. So I made the decision to simplify processes and get back to the company's roots. This decision was actually easy. Either the company would keep its great spirit alive, or it would see that spirit replaced by all these processes.

Jannis went back to a previous structure that was much simpler, more like the company had been when Kostas conceived it. This helped bring the small-company spirit back to Kofola. It made Kofola not only a better place to work but also a more innovative place to work. That's critical because the company's future depends on its ability to develop drinks that embody the Kofola spirit and appeal to a new generation.

Jannis does not want Kofola to turn into a machine that cranks out products. He concentrates on the company's ability to encourage and reward fresh thinking.

Creativity is a big reason why people love to work here. For many it is a life project. They have freedom here, more responsibility, and the space to be creative as we expand our product line.

The spirit of innovation now plays an important role in the ongoing effort to strengthen the Kofola brand. Jannis believes it's his job to empower the creative people in his company—to ensure that their work has meaning and that they have a voice in the company. These are the people whose passion and talent embody the brand, and it's their work that builds the value of the brand. By guarding against big-company behaviors, Kofola ensures that its core values prevail.

As Jannis discovered, processes and formality can take a toll on creativity, but so can the condition of the workplace itself. There came another time when Jannis had to take action to prevent big-company values from suffocating Kofola's spirit. The creative environment was being compromised as the company grew larger.

During Kofola's most successful times, Jannis observed, the work environment was fun and exciting—but not exactly neat.

Creativity can get a bit messy. There were papers and products everywhere. However, it was a place that just felt fantastic to work in.

As the company grew, a major physical change occurred. To accommodate the expanding workforce, the company moved into a larger, more contemporary building. In this new location the production manager also took on the role of office manager. Then—horror of horrors—everything became clean and organized. That was the proper atmosphere for production, but it had a chilling effect on creativity. Jannis began to feel that the workplace had lost its soul. Of course the production/office manager had the best of intentions—he wanted to create order—but the creative people did not share his values.

That experience led Jannis to embrace a new policy: Never let operations people mess with the character of an office.

Now we've gone back to the rubbish, so to speak, and the old way of working. We encourage people to be themselves. No dress code. People should work in the clothes that make them feel good. T-shirts and shorts? Why not? When people feel good, and they feel good about their workplace, they work better.

History proves that Jannis really means what he says. When he was named Entrepreneur of the Year by Ernst & Young in 2011, he had to borrow the spiffy clothes he'd need to attend the award ceremony.

Being faithful to the company's simple values has actually led to a number of awards. In 2012 Kofola won the title of most creative Czech company of the year, given by Deloitte Consulting. More recently Kofola (as a company) won Entrepreneur of the Year honors in the European Business Awards.

Jannis's determination to fight off complexity has also led to Kofola's successful expansion beyond the Czech Republic and into neighboring countries. The small-company spirit wins again.

Streamlining Is the Core of Simplicity

Leaders who simplify have a complicated task. The many obstacles they confront serve as a constant reminder that in business, simplicity is not necessarily the natural order of things.

If any one action is critical to the idea of simplification, it's the act of streamlining—taking many things and turning them into fewer things, so a business can run more fluidly.

The value of streamlining is that it actually creates something more compelling. It communicates more clearly, makes a more lasting impression, and creates focus.

The power of streamlining is evident in a product that is powerful yet easy to use. Or a product line that offers choice without confusion. Or a company that's driven by ideas instead of rule books.

Streamlining is the leader's way of shining a bright light on what's truly important. It reduces friction and encourages action.

Chapter 8
Simplicity Creates Love

This is a good time to remind ourselves why simplicity is such a powerful business force in the first place—and why leaders who operate by the principles of simplicity have such confidence in it.

No one denies that human beings are attracted to simpler things. When we see two paths to the same goal, we choose the straighter, quicker route. Not exactly rocket science.

Further, we respond warmly to the company that offers the simpler path. We start to feel some love—and the more that company delivers simpler experiences over time, the more attached we become. We grow resistant to the lure of competitors that try to steal us away.

Steve Jobs certainly built Apple's success on this principle. To him, winning the hearts of customers was the company's most important job. He made that clear every time he talked about Apple making technology that people can "fall in love with." Not only did this philosophy help drive the development of every new product, but it also built even greater anticipation for the next product. In Steve's thinking, delivering on the promise of simplicity—in products, marketing, and customer relationships—was money in the brand bank. It built an emotional connection with customers, and it was key to turning customers into evangelists who would spread the word to friends, family, and colleagues.

Steve was selling simplicity way back in Apple's earliest days. On the cover of the brochure that introduced Apple's first mainstream hit, the Apple II computer, was the headline, "Simplicity is the ultimate sophistication." At a time when computers existed only in corporate data centers, Apple offered a computer that was, yes, lovable. The belief that simplicity generates love was one of Steve's core principles and would only get stronger as he broadened the concept to include the entire user experience. Every detail was critical to Steve because every detail helped build the love. There was no room for compromise when it came to winning customers' hearts.

Like Steve, other simplicity-minded leaders put serious effort into finding new ways to continue delivering simpler experiences over time. One of the most effective ways to do this is to put oneself in the customer's shoes. This is something we should all be very good at, given that we've been customers most every day of our lives. We know the difference between a good experience and a bad one. The challenge is to be objective about the way we see our own company.

I found an interesting example of this in the world of education. Jane den Hollander, vice-chancellor at Deakin University in Melbourne, Australia, was inspired by a personal experience to push for a major simplification at her school. Jane's daughter had tried to enroll in the MBA program at a prestigious London business school, but found that she'd missed the enrollment date by just one week. Though classes weren't due to start for another three months, she was told she'd have to wait an entire year to try again. It was a devastating disappointment.

Putting herself in the shoes of her students, Jane realized that this inflexibility was built into the systems at many universities, including her own. Her experience motivated her to initiate a program that will allow enrollment through the first week of each semester. This act of simplification will offer prospective students a welcome flexibility as they juggle work, family, and education.

Such change doesn't come easy. Deakin's effort will require significant rethinking of university systems behind the scenes, but Jane believes the change will be a differentiator. It will make enrollment more sensible and demonstrate to incoming students that Deakin understands their needs. No student will ever feel the disappointment that Jane's daughter felt.

At its core, simplification is about winning the hearts of the customers, and doing everything you can to make it easy for customers to engage with you.

Simplicity, love, and profit have a perfect relationship in business. The simpler you make things for customers, the more love they feel for the company. And the more love they feel, the more business they bring.

Loving Your Friendly Local Monolith

Like banks, telecoms and cable companies aren't the types of businesses that typically inspire feelings of love. If you are Telstra in Australia or DirecTV in Latin America, you may ask yourself, "Is it even possible for customers to love a monolith, no matter how good our service might be?"

Both of these companies have strong competitors and operate in industries where customers have a long and storied history of disliking their providers.

At Telstra, Robert Nason truly believes it's possible for a monolith to win customers' hearts. After all, Telstra is the company that connects people to those who really matter in their lives at home, in school, and in business. It also delivers content that brings endless hours of entertainment into people's homes. Why can't it be loved for that?

Robert acknowledges the challenge Telstra faces in creating love. It may sell the devices people fall in love with, but since it isn't the manufacturer, it doesn't get credit for that. Its business is enabling customers to connect those devices to a network they can rely on.

Telstra aims for a different kind of love, the kind that turns customers into advocates. An advocate has a positive feeling for the company, even if it isn't the gushing kind of love people might feel for a technology or automobile brand. Robert explains:

Customers who are advocates buy more services from you than nonadvocates. They spend more money with you than nonadvocates. They churn far less than nonadvocates. So there is a commercial value in having an advocate as a customer. We're making the investment because we want our customers to become advocates.

Because access to voice and data networks has become so critical in people's lives, Telstra aims to earn its way into people's hearts by being fast, dependable, and responsive with service. The company also has an extensive program of community involvement, with initiatives to support schools, businesses, and organizations, and it is also active in disaster relief and recovery. Those activities can generate a feeling of attachment in customers and play a role in turning them into advocates.

DirecTV Latin America faces a similar challenge. CEO Bruce Churchill also acknowledges that television content providers aren't known for their ability to generate customer love.

Earning love is particularly challenging in an industry like ours. There are so many competitors, all of whom are advertising. We're selling a service, and people rely on it every day. The standard is very high, and in the world of service it's pretty hard to get people to love you.

If you look at customer-satisfaction scores, DirecTV is always the highest in pay TV. But pay TV is like the third-least-popular industry. So it's kind of a nice backhanded compliment.

DirecTV's focus is the concept of "net promoters versus net detractors," a concept similar to Nason's idea of converting customers to advocates. For DirecTV the goal is to tip the scales so that the people recommending its service (promoters) greatly outnumber those speaking against it (detractors). The biggest factors influencing positive and negative feelings are the way the company interacts with people every day and how successful it is at making customers' lives as simple as possible. Do these things well, Bruce says, and the ratio of promoters to detractors will grow.

When we talk about how the power of simplicity can generate love, it's important to understand that in business, love is a relative term, and its meaning can vary from one industry to the next. What's important is the direction in which the needle is moving. As companies find new ways to make the customer experience simpler and more rewarding, happiness and loyalty increase.

At Bank of Melbourne, chief executive Scott Tanner talked about the challenge of getting people to feel an emotional attachment to a bank. He observes that people have no problem showing love for companies that create imaginative products like electronics, cars, and clothing. But it's tougher for a bank because it must fight the stereotyped image of a business that's not exactly warm and fuzzy.

Still, Scott believes it's possible for a bank to win a place in customers' hearts. It's a matter of finding new ways to create meaningful connections with customers. After all, every bank shares the fundamental goal of helping people achieve their dreams.

It can offer advice for a young couple just starting out. It can offer support when they're starting a business or trying to grow one. It can help set up a happier retirement. When a bank does these things well, says Scott, people actually have more reason to feel an emotional connection than they do with most other companies.

As we learned earlier, Bank of Melbourne creates its version of love by linking every action to the concept of being "the local bank." It's the only bank in Victoria that has staked its future on the state's economic well-being. This makes solid business sense, because when people and organizations are successful, they save and borrow more money. Scott believes the bank can create deeper connections with customers by helping them take advantage of new opportunities.

To me, banking is about relationships and relationships are about trust. They're intimately linked. If you approach these things cynically, and your activity is just about making money for the bank, and not really helping customers, well . . . people figure that out pretty quickly.

Put another way, authenticity is what wins customers and keeps them. Bank of Melbourne positions itself as the local bank, and its behavior—taking visible interest in the community—demonstrates that the bank's "localness" isn't a marketing ploy. Customers repay authenticity with their loyalty.

In the retail industry customer love also plays a critical role, in that many stores offer identical products. There's no reason for a person to consistently choose one retailer over another unless they have warm feelings for it. So the ability to generate love can be a major factor in a retailer's success.

Love Is the New Like

After what we've heard from CEO Kip Tindell at The Container Store, you won't be surprised by the importance he places on people feeling an emotional attachment to his company. And he's talking about employees as well as customers.

People join this company and they never leave. In an industry where, on average, there is more than 100 percent turnover every year, we have historically had 10 percent or less.

Thirty-five years ago, when he was in college, Kip was moved by a belief expressed by Southwest Airlines founder Herb Kelleher: You can build a much better organization on love than you can on fear. He was talking about a new kind of management philosophy, moving away from the militaristic, top-down style.

Kip had never heard anyone talk like this. The idea fueled a lot of conversation between Kip and his roommate, John Mackey, who went on to cofound Whole Foods. They talked about the compatibility of love and business, and their passion for what they called "conscious capitalism." (Mackey wrote a book with this very title in 2013.) They thought it was not only okay to talk about love and business in the same breath but also important to do so.

Kip believes ideas like this come to life within an organization only if leadership makes them real, and that employees treated with care and concern will expand instead of contract. So he spends a significant portion of his time thanking employees—even those he doesn't know very well—for all that they do. Demonstrating commitment and appreciation helps create an environment where the workforce thrives.

But how does Kip express love for his customers, and how does he earn their love in return? He believes the answer is *value*, in the sense that the products he sells can deliver satisfaction beyond the price paid.

It's very simple, he explains: People become attached to a brand that delivers value. Kip stresses that when he talks about value, he's not necessarily talking about low price. He references retailer Stanley Marcus, of Neiman Marcus fame, who said that value is when a thing costs about 20 percent more than another but looks 200 percent better. It functions better, lasts longer, and all the while looks fantastic.

Kip uses his favorite tie as an example of value. He bought it at Bergdorf Goodman, and it's probably the most expensive tie he owns. But when he wears it, he gets tons of comments, which just makes him feel great. For him, it's the emotional return on his investment that gives him the sense of value.

We all have similar examples in our lives. We have our favorite car, our favorite shoes, and the smartphone we can't live without. These are the purchases that create an emotional response. It's natural that we feel some love for the company that made those purchases possible.

You can't achieve this response with every item you sell, says Kip. Instead what you try to do—with every sale, every product, every design, every trade show—is find things people can get emotional about. Not just things they'll like but things they can love.

> *When you have stores, you want to evoke that emotion out of all of your stakeholders. Your customers, your vendors, everyone. We joke that even our bankers and lawyers love our store.*

Kip believes in the rule of doing everything for the customer, because he believes that earning customers' love is the best business plan there is. However, he reaffirms the point that the best way to get there is by taking care of employees first.

> *The economist Milton Friedman said, "The only reason the corporation exists is to maximize the return to the shareholder."*
>
> *Well, Milton, we know you won a Nobel Prize, but we put the employee first. If you really and truly take better care of her than anyone else, she will really and truly take better care of the customer than anyone else. And if employees and customers are ecstatic, then shareholders will be ecstatic too.*

Kip's thinking has a certain similarity to that of Jack Ma, chairman of Alibaba Group Holding Limited. In a letter that was part of Alibaba's filing for what was a record-setting IPO in 2014, Ma said that his priorities were "customers first, employees second, and shareholders third," adding, "I can see that investors who hear this for the first time may find it a bit hard to understand."

While Kip and Jack may differ on exactly who comes first, they agree that shareholders are *not* priority number one. When companies focus myopically on the shareholder, employees and customers sense that, and the magic can get lost.

Another critical piece of the love puzzle for Kip is the relationship his company has with vendors. He says that his relationships are so good, sometimes it can be hard to tell the difference between the vendors and employees. The store works hard to become "the vendors' favorite customer." As a result, The Container Store gets exclusives on products, the last pallet of the hot item during the holiday season, and the best prices on the most in-demand items.

> *We're trying to create a business where everyone associated with our business thrives. The employees, the vendors, and the communities. Boy, if you do that, then you get synergy—and that's the key to making money in business.*
>
> *Business is not a zero-sum game, where one party's gain is offset by another party's loss. The companies making the most money are those creating synergies in which everyone thrives.*

Kip believes that business relationships in which one side takes advantage of the other can lead to short-term profits—but a business that operates in that manner isn't likely to endure. The only way to build a lasting, thriving business is to show love to employees and have joyful relationships with vendors.

Dave Pottruck, former CEO of Charles Schwab, also talked about the importance of emotional attachment. As a brokerage company Schwab built a relationship with customers based on trust and empowerment. To create connections the company set out to make customers feel like family—and it did that in a number of ways.

First it established that Charles Schwab wasn't just a company. He was a real person, a solid financial expert who could be trusted. He was "Chuck." Says Dave:

> *Everything in this company emanates from Chuck's personality and his personal values, so it was really important that he be visible in our advertising and be writing books and doing interviews.*

The interesting thing is, none of this came naturally to Chuck. Fundamentally he was an introvert. Cultivating a public image wasn't an easy or natural thing for him to do. But he understood the importance of being the face of the company in the effort to build love and trust. He was always willing and able to step up to play that role in an authentic way, to the best of his ability.

He was fabulous as the spokesperson for the company because he always spoke from the heart—to employees and to customers. The press loved him and continues to love him. We wanted to strengthen the affiliation people felt with our leader and our namesake.

Dave also wanted customers to feel an affiliation with employees in the local offices, as they would be the ones who directly handled people's business. Customers were encouraged to come in and get to know the staff. This was something the competition couldn't match, since they didn't have nearly as many local offices as Schwab, and most of their business was done via phone.

Even when you used Schwab's toll-free phone access, your experience was more personal than the interactions offered by competitors. If you were an active and bigger customer, you'd get your own team and your calls would always be routed to that team. That meant you'd have an ongoing relationship with people you actually knew. This enhanced Schwab's ability to create personal connections and use these connections to increase the love factor.

As the discount brokerage market matured, most of the other companies disappeared—bought out, closed down, or merged into banks. The companies that remained morphed into online brokerage services, such as E*TRADE and TD Ameritrade. But they weren't able to replicate the love customers felt for Charles Schwab, says Dave.

They tried to copy us, but they didn't appreciate that the Schwab model isn't just about having branches. What's critical is what we do in our branches—with employees who add value. That's especially important when you are charging only eight dollars for a trade. How do you make money on eight dollars? You have to be in the relationship business, and you need to attract customers with larger and larger accounts.

In Charles Schwab's case you can actually put a dollar amount to the power of love. When Dave joined Schwab, the average account was just $7,000. When he left, the average account was over $200,000. Even though the company was in a discount business with narrower margins, it increased profit by getting more customers to trust it with more money.

Like Kip Tindell, Dave talks about value leading to an emotional attachment. At Charles Schwab the ability to serve up a personal relationship in addition to discount prices created a higher level of trust, which customers perceived as real value.

In each of these cases customers found value in the product they received, whether that product was physical or conceptual. Another way to generate love may seem superficial, because technically it is not part of the product or service, but it's every bit as important. One could say it's all in the presentation.

Value + Simplicity + Design = Love

We've seen how a physical product can earn customers' love. We've seen how a sense of value can create an emotional attachment. We've also seen how even a bank can warm customers' hearts by demonstrating empathy.

But how does a company that exists entirely in the digital space create love?

StubHub cofounder Jeff Fluhr says it comes down to three things: value, simplicity, and design. A website must offer a service that truly improves people's lives, is easy to use, and is visually appealing.

StubHub didn't have a physical product, nor did it have a face-to-face relationship with its customers. It connected with people by offering a simple, well-designed site that brought fun and excitement to fans of music and sports.

Design was part of StubHub from the start. In the early days customers did receive a physical product of sorts: Actual tickets were delivered to the buyer's home. Jeff's team put a lot of effort into designing something that would leave a positive impression. They created a special StubHub ticket envelope using premium paper so customers who were already excited about going to a game or concert would have an "opening experience" at home, courtesy of StubHub.

However, creating products, packaging, and websites that connect emotionally does not come without cost. A company needs world-class designers, and hiring them can have an impact on budgets and priorities.

In my experience with Steve Jobs it was not unusual for him to exceed the budget when he saw an opportunity to create a better customer experience. He didn't need to see proof that there would be a return on investment. He simply believed that in the long run a better customer experience was worth more than the savings he might see in material cost or labor. Unfortunately, in a hypercompetitive world many companies have difficulty choosing the long term over the short term. They believe that if they don't survive in the short term, the long term is moot. While that might sound pithy and wise, it's also the thinking of a company that's aiming to survive rather than thrive.

At the time this book was written, Jeff was leading his new venture, called Spreecast. Spreecast turns a video broadcast into an interactive experience, allowing viewers to interact with the video in real time via a Twitter and Facebook stream that appears alongside. Unlimited viewers can watch and chat simultaneously, or one can create a private broadcast by invitation only.

Design plays a major role at Spreecast—but it's also a bit of a balancing act. Jeff wants the site design to be simple and beautiful, but the engineering hours necessary to achieve that are an issue when constrained by the budget of young company. Just tweaking the positioning of a graphic could potentially eat up hours of an engineer's time, says Jeff.

We go pretty damn far in making the design look great. This is one of those areas where I sometimes have to step into the product and engineering debate. Product will say, "We have to move it three pixels because it just doesn't look right." Engineering will say, "You really think more people will use our product because of those three pixels?" And product says, "Yeah."

More than once in a while, I will say, "Let's do the extra work."

Jeff has seen the proof in so many hit products: design plays a big role in creating customer love.

The Heart of Simplicity

Most business strategies are based on cold, hard facts. Simplicity is different. It's based on an understanding of human behavior. It's the acknowledgment that people have a built-in preference for a simpler experience, and when they feel that a company is providing that experience, they get attached.

Uber is a perfect example. The company has grown to provide an alternative to taxis in more than three hundred cities, its lure being a beautifully simple app that summons a reliable, affordable, comfortable ride to a customer's exact location. Your credit card is on file, so you just get in the car and go. No need to sign for the trip. It couldn't be simpler.

As Uber became a global business phenomenon, competitors sprang up claiming to offer a better alternative—a similar concept at lower prices. But, thanks to Uber's simplicity and riders' positive experiences with the service, most of its customers have remained loyal. There's little motivation to change when you're feeling the love.

The most successful companies, then, are those who find ways to "manufacture" simplicity over time, and in the process create an emotional connection.

As we've seen, no company can use size as an excuse for not making an effort to create love. Telstra and DirecTV Latin America demonstrate that even a monolith can generate warmer feelings, even if those feelings aren't exactly red-hot. The terminology may differ, but whether you are creating *advocate*s, *net promoters*, or just *fans*, you're talking about shades of the same thing. You're creating a positive emotional response in customers. You're building loyalty that will pay off more with every passing year.

By putting themselves in the customers' shoes, business leaders are finding new ways to create love by delivering simpler experiences. They're making simpler products, offering simpler choices, creating simpler advertising, and building simpler websites.

Objective measures will always play an important role in the way we evaluate business. But it's important to remember that customers value the experience as much as the products we buy—and the degree of simplicity often defines the experience.

Chapter 9
Simplicity Is Instinctive

Simplicity is a thoroughly democratic concept. It's available to everyone, and it's absolutely free. Understanding and implementing simplicity does not require a business degree.

This raises an obvious question: If simplicitiy is so powerful and so readily available, why aren't more businesses putting it to work? The best explanation is that most companies operate under a formal set of rules and don't make major decisions without hard data to support them.

A common thread among the leaders featured in this book is the belief that one must have the confidence to make a decision based on personal conviction, even if that decision might not be supported by data. They see danger in becoming too reliant on the cold, scientific part of business. They also see danger in allowing decisions to be made by committees or get mired in a sea of approvals.

This is often expressed as "acting on instinct," "guided by intuition," or "listening to one's heart." Though these phrases might imply a softer, less reliable way of working, that is not the case. Instinct is not a whim. It's developed over a lifetime, the result of years of education, experience, observation, and learning gained from triumphs and defeats.

Proponents of simplicity do not deny the value of empirical evidence. They simply believe that a business based solely on data is missing the very important human factor. Customers' behaviors, wants, needs, and desires don't always show up in spreadsheets, and when they do, they are somewhat open to interpretation.

Whole Foods CEO Walter Robb puts it this way:

I am a heart leader. In business you need to have the analytics and the disciplines and the guardrails and all that. I just think without the heart, without the real caring, you miss that greater potential of the business. It is heart that lets you strive for the humanity of a business. That's ultimately what excites and inspires people and keeps them at the company.

A similar feeling was expressed by many of the leaders with whom I spoke. They tend to look at hard numbers with suspicion, or at the very least, a feeling that numbers must be considered in a greater context. They trust their experience, and they talk about having the willingness to fly in the face of the data when their inner voice leads in a different direction. They say things like, "I believe this with every bone in my body"—which shows the importance they place on instinct.

Of course, having this kind of instinct is of little value unless one is willing to act on it. The only thing required is confidence—which is something simplicity-prone leaders seem to have in spades.

Intuition Versus Data

StubHub cofounder Jeff Fluhr has had an interesting journey. Starting with little business experience, he came to understand the power of an idea, how to strike a chord with customers, and how to turn the idea into a successful business.

When he started, however, he didn't have the intuition he has today. He says that watching people like Steve Jobs helped him develop that skill and apply it to the way he sought to connect with his own customers.

Jeff believes intuition is something one can continue to develop over time. He still "practices" today, putting his energy into understanding market trends, what consumers are doing, and what they're responding to. He observes trends in other industries and thinks about how they might be applicable to his. This knowledge gives his intuition real-world substance.

While Jeff values intuition, he does not diminish the importance of metrics. One of the advantages of a web-based business is that he can put different experiences in front of consumers and instantly see how they respond. He can experiment with different versions of headlines, images, special offers, or any other element to see which gets the best response. There is a tremendous advantage in being able to tweak and optimize one's business at the speed of the Internet.

So you could say that Jeff is a "head *and* heart" leader. He explains:

> *If you are Steve Jobs or Henry Ford, you're way ahead. I'm not anywhere near those guys and don't pretend to be. Because I can't predict the future, I tend to look at data. However, I also know that ideas and creativity lead to the products that push the world forward, like the iPhone and Facebook. So I see value in both head and heart.*

CEO Bruce Churchill of DirecTV Latin America is in a business that generates a ton of data analyzing the company's performance and customer behavior. But he thinks it's important to resist the temptation to rely too heavily on that data. In his business he sees value in listening to one's heart.

> *Metrics are just a piece of information. They're not a deciding factor. Media is not that kind of business. For most of the big moves in media, research would probably say, "Don't do it."*

As an example, Bruce talked about his days working with Rupert Murdoch, who has certainly made some bold and controversial decisions in his time. Rupert upset the status quo at the Fox network in 1993 when he bought the rights to NFL broadcasts. At that time Fox had never produced live sports at all, let alone anything as big as the NFL. The network paid what was considered a crazy amount of money—$1.6 billion for a four-year deal—yet that contract transformed Fox.

At the time, the purchase elicited such reactions as "Are you guys crazy?" and "You'll never get that money back." Today it looks like a bargain. But if Murdoch had done the traditional analysis, says Bruce, he would never have taken the plunge.

> *You can look at information that will inform your opinion. But if you think you can do research and come to an answer with total certainty, you'll be researching until the cows come home. Everyone will have left you in the dust.*
>
> *Research may work more in packaged goods, where different packaging can have an effect. That's an industry where you can take six months to make a decision. In media or technology you just don't have that kind of time.*

In other words, some of the best business decisions are made by subjecting data to the intuition test—and having the confidence to act accordingly.

Intuition Is Good Business

Ron Johnson had developed his leadership skills before he was recruited by Steve Jobs to lead Apple's retail effort. But once he joined Apple, he had an opportunity to hone his skills under the master, so to speak. To this day Ron talks about the important things he learned from his eleven years in Steve's world.

Ron believes that the best businesspeople are intuitive. They have an ability to intuit the right answer from limited information and the confidence to make decisions armed only with that information. They engage with their mind, says Ron, but they also listen to their heart.

> *By definition, spreadsheets only tell you history, right? If you rely on facts to make decisions, you'll reach the same conclusion everyone else makes based on those facts. You'll just be moving toward the middle.*
>
> *If you want to differentiate or move to the future, you have to rely on your intuition. It's like Steve Jobs said when he quoted Wayne Gretzky about skating to where the puck is going.*

Like others, Ron stresses that acting on intuition does not mean ignoring the facts. What it does mean is that you trust yourself to fill in the gaps in the information. You're looking at the data to learn all that you can but not falling into the trap of being "überanalytic." While numbers may reveal what happened, they don't necessarily tell you what to do.

The Apple Stores generated plenty of data, but Ron didn't want his team to obsess over the numbers. He felt it was far more important for them to focus on the mission—to show customers how Apple products could fulfill a need in their lives. If they did that well, the outcome would be impressive sales figures.

In a company the size of Apple, where oceans of data are pouring in every day, it's a challenge to make sure that the processing of all that data doesn't take precedence over doing the best work. As many of us know from experience, some people seem to have an innate need to churn out charts and graphs to prove they're on top of the business. They're the ones who focus on processes and not outcomes.

Part of Ron's solution was to hire people who were more mission driven than process driven. He also created a report format for the Apple retail team that was very, very simple.

> *We didn't get lost in too much data. We never let it get complicated. It was how many people came to the store, how many bought, and what did they buy? Boom, and that was it.*

It's back to simplicity—there are only a handful of metrics that you really ought to care about. Too much complex data leads to multiple versions of truth, and you want to get to that one most important version.

What Ron describes is consistent with my own experience interacting with the leadership of Apple, and a night-and-day contrast with my experience working with large companies such as Intel and Dell. It's far more typical for big organizations to emphasize head over heart. In those complicated companies, literally no project begins without a spreadsheet that proves an immediate return on investment. No major advertising idea is approved without extensive focus-group testing and revisions. While that may sound like a solid way to approach business, it negates the benefits of instinct that come from years of leadership and experience.

For that reason I was fascinated when Robert Nason of Telstra shared his feelings about head versus heart. When you're a giant public company with so many shareholders and analysts watching over you, says Robert, it's tough to rationalize any decision based largely on heart.

Nevertheless, at Telstra there is an understanding that different initiatives can call for different approaches. For example, when the company seeks to improve the customer experience with an existing product or service, it studies focus groups and customer feedback. It discovers what things customers like to do most. It finds out how happy they are with their devices and accessories. When it's trying to improve something that currently exists, that kind of feedback is useful and necessary.

But there are also initiatives at Telstra aimed at providing customers with capabilities they can't imagine, and testing in these instances would be of limited or no use. The company must have the freedom to experiment. It must encourage people to come up with new ideas and give them the space to try new things. That's where the heart comes in. Says Robert:

We'll have a crack and see if it works. We'll put teams together and have a go at something and see how well it rolls out. These can be very small initiatives or big ones.

Being unburdened by excessive data is a simpler way to work. Robert shared an example of a project that was done as an experiment, coming purely from the heart and not in response to any customer feedback. This project ended up creating one of Telstra's most notable successes.

Concerned about the number of bushfires in Australia, a Telstra employee suggested that the company develop a system for authorities that would send an SMS to everyone in a geographic location, warning them to evacuate when a fire was approaching. Telstra developed this technology and then rolled it out to all customers at no charge, helping make everyone safer during bushfire season.

No one needed to run a P&L or start researching the viability of producing a bushfire warning system, because Telstra's executive team knew in their hearts it was the right thing to do. It became one more reason for people to feel a little love for Telstra.

Robert, and so many of the business leaders I spoke to, made a connection between a company's willingness to act from the heart and its ability to create a simpler business in the eyes of employees and customers. It's the excessive reliance on data, or an unwillingness to act without a mountain of data, that often adds layers of complexity, even when the intention is to make things run more smoothly.

A leader who has the confidence to lead with heart has the ability to keep data and processes in their proper place.

Numbers Can't Rule Your Life

Since my background is in a creative business, I was gratified to hear so many business leaders talk about the need to absorb data, but not let it dictate decisions.

John McGrath flatly states that you can't engage human beings when your business is based solely upon hard numbers. He describes his approach as 90 percent heart and 10 percent head. Of course he looks at research, but if the numbers say something that flies in the face of his instinct, he has no problem saying, "Sorry, I don't agree with those figures." Says John:

Numbers can sort of sway you in one direction or another. I don't ignore
them. That would be craziness. But I certainly don't let them rule my life.
They're just a small factor in a decision.

Even though instinct is a human characteristic, John believes people
are born with varying degrees of it. Like Jeff Fluhr, he thinks we can get
better at it through experience, observation, and curiosity. But just as instinct can be sharpened over time, it can also fade if we don't give it proper
exercise. Given the size and success of McGrath, John's instincts have
clearly served him well.

His combination of instinct and confidence has dampened his enthusiasm for certain traditional ways of doing business. For example, most of
the bigger companies in the real estate industry make extensive use of focus
groups. John believes focus groups can be skewed based on the questions
one asks, so this type of research doesn't always yield a true read. He feels
that experience is a better gauge.

Without sounding too arrogant, I think I know what people want, almost
to a point more than they know. I know what customers want when
they're selling property, because I've been doing this for so long. I know
what a great experience looks and sounds like. I know how to deliver that.

Since people don't buy a house all that often, John feels there would be
limited value in asking them for opinions about the process. What comes
out of focus groups is "mostly the basic garbage." He believes focus group
respondents typically come up with things that should be common knowledge for anyone in the industry who is good at their job.

As an example, John talks about "price guides" in real estate listings.
When a residential property is put up for auction, there is no set price. If
McGrath believes—based on its expertise—that the property will ultimately be sold for between $900,000 and $1 million, it will put that price
guide in its listing. Most real estate agents in Australia don't do this. They
simply note that there will be an auction and provide a date for it.

If a prospective home buyer calls to ask, "What do you think it will go for?" the agent will say, "We're not really sure. Why don't you come and take a look at it?"

John thinks that's outrageous. He doesn't need a focus group to tell him it's outrageous. It's purely instinctive, based on his experience in the business and his knowledge of human behavior. As a customer he'd never want to waste his time looking at properties he couldn't afford. So he directs his agents to discuss pricing with a seller and get approval to add a price guide to the listing. This is simply a courtesy to buyers, and it's one more way to treat them with respect.

> *It seems like such a basic thing. I mean, you're probably hearing this and thinking, "Well, duh." But this is what our industry does. I think that's insanity. I can't imagine why we'd ever have to discuss it, let alone engage in research about it.*

I very much enjoyed the way some of these topics set off the feisty side of John McGrath. We all see things going on in our business that add little value and waste too much time. It's uplifting to hear a leader place such importance on instinct and have the strength to put it into action. Like many of the leaders you've met in this book, John is simply trying to give his customers the best possible user experience. He's not looking for ways to "reel in" new customers with tricky ploys.

John used his instinct to arrive at a philosophy for social media as well. The company has a Facebook page, but that page contains no listings of properties for sale. John's thinking is that this needs to be a place where the company can nurture relationships with customers—talking about the latest trends, fresh designs, some cool property that's just been built overseas, the hottest architects, etc. It's about furthering the image of McGrath as the premium seller of residential homes and an authority that lives and breathes real estate. If, on the other hand, someone wants to buy a property, that's what the company's main website is for. John explains:

This has really resonated well. But again, I didn't need to stage a focus group to know it was the right way to go. People come to our website to look at our properties. They come to our Facebook page for opinion, guidance, wisdom, and some gut feelings about things.

Some marketing people said we should be pushing product on our Facebook page, and I just said, "No, we're not going to do that." I don't need research to prove it, and I don't need to debate it. Our social media site is for connecting with customers and building our brand.

John's examples demonstrate that acting on one's instinct can cut out weeks of agonizing over largely pointless analysis. Business moves faster and strategies get smarter when they're based on real-world knowledge and the wisdom that comes with experience.

Like John, Ted Chung believes businesses that put too much emphasis on research and data are missing something very important.

Emotions, Not Numbers

At its core Hyundai Card is a financial operation, and numbers certainly can't be ignored. However, vice chairman Ted Chung firmly believes that human understanding is what differentiates Hyundai Card from its competitors. In the discussion of head versus heart, he puts his faith firmly in the heart.

While my college major was literature, I went to MIT—where everything is numbers. It's probably because I played with numbers so much at the university that I found myself wanting to know the things that numbers cannot tell you.

Ted explains that many of the decisions we make in life are more emotional than rational. When we buy a car, for example, we look at price, maintenance cost, resale value, and other hard bits of information. In the end, however, the decision is often about more than just numbers. It's about lifestyle, enjoyment, and how the car makes us feel.

For this reason Ted believes it would be foolish for Hyundai Card to make decisions based solely on numbers. As a responsible leader he must study the data, but he uses it mainly to get a sense of his customers' needs and desires and better understand how they like to live.

> *I cannot do real crazy things. But we can and do make our decisions based on our passion. I often ask my team to ignore the numbers, and instead we'll talk about what we* want *to do and what we* can *do. We talk about the kind of company we want to be. We have to be honest.*

Ted is proud that he's hired people who have such passion for their work, and he encourages people to work in a way they find comfortable. He doesn't want to hold them to rigid ways of doing things and encourages them to think like human beings rather than machines. His view is that a business—even one devoted to finance—needs to make an emotional connection with customers. To do that it must understand and celebrate what human beings really care about.

For that reason, he believes marketing is one of the most effective ways to communicate the company's values, and so much of marketing is visual. Just as many of our lifetime attachments are based on visual images (people, places, homes, etc.), a big part of what we feel about a company is the result of what we see. So it can't be about numbers alone. Ted believes that design is important not only in creating the office environment and developing new products, but it is critical to marketing as well. It must create an image in the mind of the customer.

> *The age of advertising is over. The age of expression is here—and when it comes to expression, design is one of the most important elements. That's why I put such an emphasis on that here, even though people thought it was crazy, especially in the finance business and especially at a time when we were losing so much money.*

When he talks about the importance of image, Ted is talking about something far removed from the world of spreadsheets and financial research. He speaks and leads from his inner beliefs. When he talks about the reasons for the company's success over the last decade, it's about creativity, design, and, most of all, human understanding. It is absolutely not about a slavish devotion to numbers.

Instinct as the Great Simplifier

While they agree that data can yield valuable insights, the leaders who spoke in this chapter stress that instinct is essential to running and simplifying a business. It brings in the human perspective.

Instinct comes from both business experience and life experience. It's accumulated wisdom, personal conviction, empathy, humor, common sense, and more. It's knowing "in our bones" what path to take when there is partial or even contradictory evidence.

Westpac's Brian Hartzer, echoing the thoughts of Jeff Fluhr and Robert Nason, says that head versus heart is not an either/or proposition. In a big bank, management depends on metrics to provide a sense of the company's direction. Data helps diagnose what parts of the machine aren't working well enough or pinpoint opportunities where performance needs to be improved.

But Brian believes that one of the most important things he can do is see the banking experience through the eyes of the customer, and that's more about heart. He argues that banking is an emotional business and not an objective one, because money is tied up in people's heads. It's part of their identity. The way a bank acts has an impact on customers' notions of self-worth, identity, and their sense of security and personal control.

Because the bank deals in this emotional zone, Brian tries to structure the bank's products and policies in such a way as to eliminate confusion and doubt at those important moments when people have to make a critical financial decision. This is the only way to create a genuine connection with customers, and it is only tangentially affected by research.

While Brian talks about the value of head and heart, Joe Mimran attributes the success of Joe Fresh entirely to instinct. That's largely because he's in the fashion business, but also because he believes in good business. You would think that the risky strategy of launching a new brand inside supermarkets would demand focus groups and deep analysis. But Joe says it was *not* doing those things that set his brand apart. He well remembers how it all started.

> *No marketing studies. Just instinct. I think you need to have intuition to differentiate, and differentiating is critical. Because if you take a look at your competitors and compete on their terms, that's where you run into trouble. Differentiating is exactly what we did—by instinct alone.*

We've heard from a number of leaders in disparate industries (technology, groceries, real estate, credit cards, fashion) who proudly talk about their ability to look beyond the data. Intuition, in effect, is an essential part of their business plan.

Listening to one's heart is not a sign of weakness. Quite the opposite. It often takes courage to make decisions based on a gut feeling when so many businesses rely on science and process. But these are the decisions that often lead to a simpler company and a deeper relationship with customers.

Chapter 10
Finding Your Road to Simple

In the previous pages you've gotten a glimpse into the thinking of more than forty business leaders who credit simplicity as a driver of their success. That's terrific for them, but far more important is what's in it for you.

Ideas can only take you so far. What you really need is a plan. So what's the best way to start simplifying within your own company or department?

I suggest starting by taking some cues from the leaders who have told their stories in this book. The basic fact is, most companies can't be changed overnight. The best way to approach simplification, especially in complex organizations, is to be methodical and take it one step at a time. One must build support for the effort.

Every company is unique. Yours may sell physical products, provide services, or exist entirely on the Internet. You might do business in one city or span the globe. There is no such thing as a one-size-fits-all road map to simplicity.

Instead consider this your road map to developing a road map—an outline of strategies to consider and actions you might take as you set out to leverage the power of simplicity.

Commit

Bringing simplicity into a company isn't a part-time job. Simplification requires more energy than you might imagine. You may well have to deal with those who are skeptical, resistant, or—even worse—actively opposed. That's why the first requirement for implementing simplicity is commitment.

JCPenney's misadventure can be attributed at least partially to a lack of commitment. The company started down a radical path and then abandoned ship. Years later it still hasn't recovered. Who knows where it would be today if it had stuck to the plan that had all the experts so excited at the start.

Commitment is the key when trying to simplify a company of any size. At Australia's biggest telecom, Telstra, the simplification process took root because it had the firm backing of leadership. That commitment was visible to the workforce, raising morale and inviting participation.

Is your company committed to simplification? Will management stand by the decisions, even if those decisions ruffle some feathers?

Pick Your Team

If yours is a small company, simplification might be something you can manage by yourself. If you're part of a bigger, more complicated organization, you'll likely need a team. In this case you should ask, "Who do I want in the boat with me when the going gets tough?"

Your team needs to understand the challenges ahead, and they can't be shy when it comes time to put stakes in the ground. You'll want to be uncompromising in execution, so start by being uncompromising in your choice of teammates.

Think about the specific expertise of the people you choose. Depending on the size of your company, you might want to include people from different departments. Most important is that your team share the commitment to simplification and be willing to take a fresh look at every part of the business. A little skunkworks attitude goes a long way.

Have a Mission

The mission is a powerful tool for keeping a company on track, serving as a guideline for decisions, behaviors, and product development.

Does your company have one? Is it concise and inspirational? It might be time to create one or take a closer look at the mission you already have and update it if necessary.

Recall how Ron Johnson powered the Apple Stores with the idea of "enriching lives." Remember also that Jeff Fluhr launched StubHub without even thinking of a mission statement, but came to understand that a mission was necessary for the company's growth. And heed the lesson of Ben & Jerry's, which built a remarkable (and simple) brand by putting its mission front and center.

A mission doesn't have to be formalized, framed, or saluted. But it does have to be known. When the workforce has internalized the mission, it unifies—and as it does, it simplifies.

Observe

In the role of simplifier you'll be taking a cold, hard look at (a) your company's organization, (b) its processes, and (c) the customer experience.

Required equipment: eyes, ears, and a notepad.

This was Steve Jobs's technique before he was even named Apple's interim CEO. He talked to key people inside and outside the company and took plenty of notes on how people experienced the company and its work. Those notes became the basis of his recommendations to the executive board.

Go talk to people. Get a sense of what excites them and what frustrates them. Some topics you might want to explore:

Does the workforce embrace the mission? It's one thing for managers to be able to recite the company's mission, but how well does the workforce understand it? How deeply is it embedded in the culture? Having a mission is more fulfilling than having a job.

Have processes become too complicated? Have they become too rigid? How long do things take? Complex processes tend to dilute ideas, frustrate employees, and waste both time and money. Remember, you're not trying to solve the problem here. You're just trying to understand it.

Is the decision maker part of the process? Do people feel like they're getting input from the decision maker, or are they hearing his or her thoughts secondhand? Having that person involved from the start not only saves time but also can be inspirational, as Brian Hartzer demonstrated in the results he achieved at Westpac Bank.

How long do employees stay with the company? Complexity reveals itself in higher turnover numbers.

How do people feel on Monday mornings? When employees are fresh and eager to attack on Monday mornings, that's a very good sign. If they're not inspired to go to work each week, it's likely that complexity is taking its toll.

Involve

Big change is often difficult to sell to the rank and file. Not so with simplicity. It's a major change that comes with instant support. Simplicity is what people want; complexity drives them away.

Take advantage of that.

Lay out your plans. Don't just ask the workforce to support your changes—urge them to become part of the transformation and to suggest new ideas that further the cause. Reward them for participating.

We learned from leaders in big banks and telecoms that some of the best ideas for simplification originate within the workforce. At Whole Foods, Walter Robb described how the company's policy of motivating and empowering employees helps fulfill the mission of promoting a healthier lifestyle and a healthier planet.

Simplification isn't business as usual, and it isn't merely a dictate from above. It needs to become a part of the culture.

Be the Customer

There is only one true judge of how simple your business is—your customer. As the simplifier in chief, you need to put yourself in the customer's shoes and evaluate the total experience.

If you're brutally honest about what you see and feel, it's not hard to spot the complexities that tarnish the experience. This is how the leaders in large companies like Telstra and DirecTV went about the task of simplifying, and it's how a start-up like StubHub kept its business simple as it grew.

A few basic questions to ask yourself:

Is the journey consistent? Look at the entire experience—before, during, and after the customer makes a purchase or orders a service. Look at what your customer experiences when interacting with your advertising, PR, website, retail stores, packaging, technical support, etc. Map it out. Is there a consistent message throughout? A consistent set of values? A consistent visual style?

Would the total experience make you an evangelist? Is your company providing a total customer experience that's so good, you'd go out of your way to rave to friends, family, or colleagues? Or would you hesitate to do so? If so, why?

What are you selling? Are the choices more confusing than clarifying? Are the differences among your products significant enough that customers find it easy to choose? Are all of your products consistent with the company's mission?

Is your marketing focused? Or are customers getting too many messages for any one of them to really sink in? Does every ad align with the mission and enhance the brand?

Does your website achieve "flow"? Does it invite visitors to follow an instinctual path as they navigate your pages? Or are you packing it all in just because you can? Even a well-designed distraction is still a distraction.

Does your retail presence tell your story? If you make physical products, does your packaging reflect your company's values? Design speaks loudly. Tiffany's distinctive blue packaging, for example, speaks loudly about the brand's timeless elegance. A brown cardboard box wouldn't quite do.

Are you selling or building relationships? Do customers feel attached to your company after their first interaction? Are you curating an attachment or ignoring it?

Empower

It's both fascinating and ironic to note that when Apple was floundering to reestablish itself as an innovator, the keys to the company's recovery—Jony Ive and his design group—had actually been on the premises all along. They had simply been marginalized as the company grew more complicated. By empowering this group, Steve Jobs ignited Apple's historic resurgence.

Robert Nason used a similar approach to empower his employees when undertaking the simplification at Telstra. With a new focus on customer service, Robert raised the profile of the people who were directly interacting with customers. By giving them a louder voice and a stake in the simplification process, he helped Telstra focus on creating a better customer experience.

Empowering those who can make a difference really makes a difference.

Clarify

We looked at the concept of choice and how in many businesses too much choice can do more harm than good. Your product offering is one place where simplicity can shine the brightest.

Recall how Westpac's credit card sales went up when the choices went down. Overlapping options can easily confuse.

Ideally you make every product because you should, not because you can. Offering fewer choices doesn't make you less of a company. On the contrary, it can convince customers you truly understand their needs.

Consider also that the presentation is as important as the products themselves. Even a complex product line can be presented in a simpler way. Remember, it's the perception of simplicity that sticks with customers.

Think also about the names you put on products —they speak volumes about what you sell, giving customers something to relate to and remember. How well can you relate to a Blu-ray player called the Sony BDPS3200? Or a laptop called the ASUS E402MA? Again, see your offerings through the customer's eyes.

Every time you make things simpler for customers, you're building love.

Aim High

Incremental improvements are a good and healthy thing. If a business isn't constantly improving, something is seriously wrong.

But this is no time for thinking small. If you want to inspire change, it has to be inspiring. A lofty vision for a simpler company will ignite passions and motivate the workforce to participate.

Swim Upstream

In many companies employees sometimes get nostalgic about "the good old days" when everything seemed simpler. More often than not, it really *was* simpler—and not just because the company was smaller.

Westpac CEO Brian Hartzer got it exactly right when he talked about the need to swim upstream to get a picture of how things worked before all the smart people made their additions and refinements. Some improvements are necessary and valuable, but others may only be adding layers of complexity.

Head upstream to find a less complicated state of operations. Isolate the things that have been tacked on over the years and reevaluate how much they really add to your business.

Streamline

Streamlining is the antidote to complexity, and few companies lack opportunities to streamline. There are many obvious places to choose from, like processes and product offerings. But look deeper, because complexity has a way of spreading its wings.

Streamline your marketing. Many companies dilute their marketing efforts by splitting their audience into too many segments. That can drain resources quickly.

Are you trying to say too many things to too many people? Or can you concentrate your resources on a single bold message that addresses a wider audience? Overanalysis is a frequent cause of unnecessary complication.

Streamline your org chart. Look at your entire organization through the lens of simplicity. What's always been there doesn't necessarily need to be there. Plenty of companies have downsized during tough times only to discover that they ran more efficiently with a streamlined organization. Overstaffed departments and overlapping responsibilities waste money and breed complexity.

Streamline approvals. How many layers does an idea have to travel through before it gets approved? How early in the process does the final decision maker get involved? In organizations that value simplicity, that decision maker is involved from day one. Bringing him or her in at the very end of the process is a recipe for frustration and wasted time.

Think Like a Start-up

One of the values shared by the leaders in this book is a respect for the entrepreneurial spirit, even in companies that are huge by every practical measure. They have a common disdain for complex internal structures, heavy processes, and unnecessary meetings. They understand that these are big-company trappings that ultimately drive people away.

Think about eliminating the middlemen. Scott Tanner at the Bank of Melbourne wasn't interested in seeing layers of employees beneath his managers. He wanted to see his managers roll up their sleeves and be hardworking members of the team.

Don't be afraid to streamline your organization into something that more resembles a start-up. A small-company mind-set can be an effective driver of big-company success.

Trust Yourself

Those who lead for simplicity show quite a bit of confidence in their own instinct. They should. They have a lifetime of knowledge and experience to draw from, and they're experts in their field.

Ted Chung led a renaissance in a business that's all about numbers, but his success came from his sense of humanity. John McGrath felt that he knew his customers better than they knew themselves, and used his instinct to rise above his competition. Kip Tindell rejected traditional business values because he believed in the possibilities of a company with heart.

Data can be your friend—just remember who's the boss. Numbers are powerful, but so is the wealth of experience you have to draw from, not just as a businessperson, but as a human being.

Be a Designer

One of the biggest business stories of our time is the rise of design. Thanks to multiple product revolutions and increasing appreciation for the value of design, consumers now demand it. Companies today not only profit by designing better products and services but also excel by looking at their own organizations with an eye for design.

When we talk about simplification, that's exactly what we're talking about: a better-designed company. Look at your organization as a machine with many moving parts, and design them to work together flawlessly without waste and without frustration.

The best way to assess the design of your company is to embrace the words of French writer Antoine de Saint-Exupéry, who said, "Perfection is reached not when there is nothing left to add, but when there is nothing left to take away."

Most companies have plenty to take away. Sometimes it's obvious, and other times it's well hidden. The goal is to do more with fewer parts and choose the straight line over the long and winding road.

Simplicity is the foundation of a well-designed company. If you design well, you win the hearts of employees and customers. Because, as we know, simplicity is easy to love.

Only the Determined Need Apply

I opened this book by explaining that simplicity isn't simple. A couple hundred pages later I stand by that statement.

Not a single business leader we heard from suggested that simplifying is as easy as issuing an executive order. Making a company simpler typically requires steely determination, a touch of relentlessness, and marathon-like endurance.

There's only one reason why any sane leader would launch such an initiative: It's worth it.

Simplicity can be the difference between success and struggle, between fulfillment and frustration, between growth and stagnation. It can make companies and it can make careers. I have no doubt—especially after spending time with the leaders in this book—that simplicity is the most powerful force in business.

You will no doubt experience bumps and bruises as you guide your business on the journey to a simpler place. But with energy and determination you will change minds. What starts as an initiative inside your company can easily turn into a movement.

Steve Jobs never diminished the challenge of simplification. He talked about how hard it was to be simple. But in the same breath he said that once you achieve simplicity, "you can move mountains."

He wasn't talking about himself. He was talking about you. The philosophy he expressed can be embraced by anyone, in any company, in any industry. To begin, you only need to put your stake in the ground.

Best of luck moving your mountains.

Share Your Simplification

In this book you've heard thoughts about simplification from business leaders around the world in a range of industries. Some found ways to keep things simple as their small companies grew bigger. Others found ways to eliminate the complexities that had taken hold in big, established companies.

However, I'm missing one very important story: yours.

I'm eager to hear how other companies have found ways to leverage the power of simplicity. I'd love to share your ideas and methods with readers on my website, in presentations around the world, and in future books.

If your company has made gains via simplification, congratulations. I know how much work it was. Let's use your story to inspire others. Write soon!

Ken Segall
simplestories@kensegall.com

A Heartfelt Thanks

I'm indebted to the many business leaders who generously gave their time to make this book possible. Your inspiration is so very appreciated.

Anderson, Laura | Chairman, Strategic Vision Global, Melbourne, Australia

Barnett, Christian | Creative Strategist, London, UK

Bassat, Andrew | Cofounder & CEO, SEEK, Sydney, Australia

Beard, Randall | CMO, Nielsen Company, New York, NY, USA

Chang, Art | Founder & CEO, Tipping Point Partners, New York, NY, USA

Chrétien, Gérard | Managing Director, Focal Speakers, La Talaudière, France

Chung, Ted | CEO, Hyundai Card, Seoul, South Korea

Churchill, Bruce | CEO, DirecTV Latin America, New York, NY, USA

den Hollander, Jane | Vice-Chancellor & President, Deakin University, Melbourne, Australia

Due Jensen, Niels | Chairman, Grundfos, Bjerringbro, Denmark

Feldman, Konrad | CEO, Quantcast, New York, NY, USA

Fluhr, Jeff | Cofounder, StubHub, San Francisco, CA, USA

Greenfield, Jerry | Cofounder, Ben & Jerry's Ice Cream, Burlington, VT, USA

Hartzer, Brian | CEO, Westpac Bank, Sydney, Australia

Hayden, Steve | Former Vice Chairman, Ogilvy, New York, NY, USA

Higgins, Colin | Associate Professor & MBA Program Director, Deakin Business School, Melbourne, Australia

Johnson, Ron | Founder & CEO, Enjoy, Menlo Park, CA; Former VP of Retail, Apple, Cupertino, CA, USA

Kamen, Jon | Cofounder & Partner, RadicalMedia, New York, NY, USA

Kroll, Jules | Chairman, K2 Intelligence, New York, NY, USA

McGrath, John | CEO, McGrath, Sydney, Australia

Mills, Steven | Executive VP of Software & Systems, IBM, Armonk, NY, USA

Mimran, Joe | Fashion Designer, Joe Fresh Fashions, New York, NY, USA

Nason, Robert | Former Group Executive of Business Support and Improvement, Telstra, Sydney, Australia

Neider, Bryan | COO, Electronic Arts, Menlo Park, CA, USA

Olivo, Allen | VP of Marketing, PayPal, San Jose, CA, USA

Pottruck, Dave | Former President & CEO, Charles Schwab, San Francisco, CA, USA

Rechler, Scott | Chairman & CEO, RXR Realty, New York, NY, USA

Robb, Walter | CEO, Whole Foods, Austin, TX, USA

Ross-Steffey, Letha | VP of Studio Partnerships, AMC Theatres, Leawood, KS, USA

Scherma, Frank | Cofounder & Partner, RadicalMedia, Los Angeles, CA, USA

Sellars, Kevin | Former VP of Advertising & Digital Marketing, Intel, Santa Clara, CA, USA

Silverman, Mark | Entrepreneur, Denver, CO, USA

Sonnenfeld, Stephen | VP of Marketing, Thomson Reuters, Stamford, CT, USA

Suiter, Tom | Tom Suiter Creative, Woodside, CA, USA

Tanner, Scott | CEO, Bank of Melbourne, Melbourne, Australia

Tischler, Howard | Founder & CEO, EverSafe, Columbia, MD, USA

Tindell, Kip | Chairman & CEO, The Container Store, Coppell, TX, USA

Wilhite, Steve | Former VP of Marketing, Apple, Cupertino, CA, USA

Wink, Chris | CEO & Chief Creative Officer, Blue Man Group, New York, NY, USA

Wood, Tom | Cofounder & Partner, Foolproof, London, UK

Acknowledgments

In his 2005 Stanford commencement speech Steve Jobs said, "You can't connect the dots looking forward; you can only connect them looking backwards."

Exhibit A: my life. No way in hell I could have connected the dots looking forward, but in a strange way it all makes sense looking back.

I learned the basics of business working at my uncle's hot dog stand on the Jersey shore when I was a teenager. Thank you, Ed Segall. Years later, when I was having doubts about my future as a rock drummer, a fellow hot dog professional (by that time an ad agency pro) inspired me to get a day job in advertising. Thank you, Martha Mosko D'Adamo.

When Chiat\Day LA was looking for a production department gopher, I was the right gopher for the job. There I met the legendary Jay Chiat, along with Steve Hayden and Lee Clow, who were cranking out Apple's award-winning advertising (including the famous "1984" commercial).

Somehow that all led to me working as a writer on Apple, then on NeXT, and then back on Apple again. No sane person could possibly have planned this out, but it happened. So a huge thanks to Chiat, Jobs,

Acknowledgments

Hayden, Clow, the creative people, account people, and clients I was priviledged to work with. They all fueled my fascination with simplicity and all of them have influenced the ideas put forward in this book.

And then there are a number of people to whom I express gratitude for their specific contributions.

- *Mary Martin, wizard of research.* Mary was born with some kind of internal simplicity sensor, for which I am forever indebted.
- *Ellie Schwartz, social media expert.* Actually, that's her day job. By night she was chief (and only) transcriber of my interviews. I'm afraid to count up the hours she spent. A thousand thanks, Ellie.
- *Natalie Horbachevsky, editor and magician.* Natalie has a gift for arranging thoughts in a way that my little brain cannot. I appreciate her sticking with me from start to finish, through thick and thin.
- *Adrian Zackheim, publisher of Portfolio.* Without Adrian's confidence and support, this book simply wouldn't exist. Heck, it might not even have a title.
- *Craig Frazier, illustrator and storyteller.* Craig put pen to sketch pad (literally) and came up with the *Think Simple* cover design. What an amazing talent. I'm honored that he was so eager to work on my book.
- *Neil Lowenbraun and Elizabeth Gordon.* I thank this dynamic duo for general support, for years of friendship, and for orchestrating some key connections.
- *Stew Kennedy.* My secret agent in Sydney and general guide to the unknown, who has connected me with some of the most fascinating people Down Under.
- *Jac Phillips.* Not only one of Melbourne's kindest and most helpful souls, Jac also is the current record holder for the most times having endured an *Insanely Simple* presentation. By far.
- *Jeremy Segall.* Yes, that's my kid. Three years ago, he outsimplified the old man by offering up the words *Think Simple.* Why didn't I think of that?

- *Kylie Wright-Ford, chief operating and strategy officer at World 50.* Kylie's advice and connections early in the research stage are greatly appreciated.
- *Zita Segall Neto.* It helps when your sister is an expert copy editor, grammarian, and sounding board. Much better than having to pay someone too. Let it be known that Zita's services are available in both English and Portuguese! She's also a proud member of . . .
- *The* Think Simple *Proofreading Squad.* The same crew that scoured my first book signed on for another tour of duty. Joining Zita were Michael Rylander, Tom Witt, and Valerie Hausladen—plus this year's rookies, Ellie Schwartz and former brewmaster Sam Behrend.
- *Christy Fletcher.* I'm forever indebted to my amazing literary agent for her ability to see a glimmer of hope in a first-time author some four years ago. (Me.) She's a fountain of knowledge, always available for an opinion, and a frequent source of moral support.
- *Friends and family.* I apologize to all for disappearing for extended periods during the process of researching and writing. You know who you are—I just hope you remember who I am.
- Last, I am compelled to say it again. Thank you to the business leaders who donated their valuable time to take part in this book—the most inspirational group of people I've ever met.

Index

Index